THE TRUTH IS SENSATIONAL ENOUGH

MERCER
UNIVERSITY PRESS

Endowed by
TOM WATSON BROWN
and
THE WATSON-BROWN FOUNDATION, INC.

THE TRUTH IS SENSATIONAL ENOUGH

Meditations for the Church Year

JIM DANT

Mercer University Press
Macon, Georgia

MUP/P364
ISBN 978-0-88146-064-3

© 2007 Mercer University Press
1400 Coleman Avenue
Macon, Georgia 31207
All rights reserved

First Edition.

Books published by Mercer University Press are printed on acid free paper that meets the requirements of American National Standard for Information Sciences—Permanence of Paper for Printed Library Materials.

Library of Congress Cataloging-in-Publication Data

Dant, James C., 1961-
The truth is sensational enough : meditations for the church year / James Dant. -- 1st ed.
p. cm.
ISBN-13: 978-0-88146-064-3 (pbk. : alk. paper)
ISBN-10: 0-88146-064-8 (pbk. : alk. paper)
1. Church year meditations. I. Title.
BV30.D36 2007
242'.3—dc22
2007012139

For

Lauryn, Meggie, and Holly,

who bring joy to my holidays…and my "everydays."

CONTENTS

ACKNOWLEDGMENTS

I've never lost my patience with award recipients. You know the ones. They reach into a pocket or purse to retrieve a folded piece of paper that holds the names of those who made the moment possible. The initial names are usually well known: God, the Lord Jesus, Dad and Mom and more. The later names are more obscure.

The recipients read and cry and read until the music begins to play and the microphone slowly descends into the floor—sure signs the audience, corporate sponsors, and producers have heard all they want to hear. I've never lost my patience with these litanies of gratitude, however, because I value the support I've received through the years.

All of the names I will mention here were integral to the completion of this book. Some know the value of their contribution. Others, however, may be surprised to find their names listed. Indulge me for a moment while I unfold my list of names.

My deep gratitude goes to Johnette Wesley Walker—my fifth grade teacher on whom I had an enormous crush and for whom, now, years later, I have the highest respect. She taught me—forced me—to outline chapters in a social studies textbook. (She could have told me to learn calculus and I would have given it my best shot for her!) Teaching me to organize thoughts and themes became an invaluable part of my life's work and this particular project.

I owe a debt of gratitude to Don Parker, Estil Jones, Wade Huie, and Truett Gannon, whose words and notes of critique and encouragement have, over the years, conveyed to me the value of the preaching moment. They also contributed much to my personal sense of value within the preaching moment.

Carol Brown, Debbie Buchanan, and Marc Jolley deserve some level of beatification. They not only had to listen to these sermons, but they were then willing to listen again (and again…and again), applying their editorial pens and perspectives to help make these spoken words readable. They are now officially saints.

As always, my undying gratitude goes to the coffee shop gang at Barnes &Noble: Debbie, Jamie, Katy Bug, Marcus, Andrew, Samantha, Kitty, Tripp, Nickie, Courtney, and Shawn. They kept the caffeine coming and called me by name every time I stepped into the store. Their names are important to me as well.

Over the last thirty years, the congregations of Highland Hills Baptist Church, Baxley's First Baptist Church, Marietta's First Baptist Church, Mt. Olivet Baptist Church, Parkwood Hills Baptist Church, Madisonville's First Baptist Church, and Northside Baptist Church have allowed me to find my particular voice—maybe even find myself—in their pulpits. Hopefully we're all better for having shared the time.

And finally, my deepest word of thanks goes to my family. I'm certain they have tired of broken conversations from a computer keyboard. But they have graciously given me the time and encouragement necessary to have this conversation with you.

PREFACE

I have broken all Ten Commandments in the process of writing this book.

I. Every writer's manuscript, at some point, becomes a god.

II. I have never carved an idol from stone or wood, but I make a habit of carving images…imaginations…with words. Some of the heavenly images I propose may disturb you. Some of them disturb me. I'm willing to give account to the Creator for any ill use of the creative ability with which I've been blessed.

III. I reluctantly use a computer. It is inevitable that power surges, improper keystrokes, and technological glitches cause the loss of files. Thus, it is inevitable that this commandment be broken.

IV. While attending Sabbath services at Temple Beth Israel, the inspiration of a note or notion has often prompted me to pick up a pencil and jot a thought for inclusion in this work. Oops.

V. My parents did not want me to be a preacher or a writer. Oops again.

VI. Following my delivery of one of the sermons published in this book, a parishioner told me that my interpretation of the biblical text was well executed. I was afraid to ask exactly what she meant.

VII. If the simplest definition of adultery is "misplaced affection," then I am guilty. I have not slept with women other than my wife, but there have been nights when the pages of this manuscript were laid between my wife and me on our sheets.

VIII. There is far too much hoopla today over the plagiarism of sermon ideas and content. I confess: I've never had an original idea. All of my sermons have some connection to the written text of biblical literature. Most of my sermons were birthed from a line or an idea or a tone delivered by some other insightful and inspired human being. So, if you find one of your sermons, sermon lines, or sermon ideas in the pages of this book, consider it a compliment...and not a crime. Then, go compliment the person from whom you stole it.

IX. The minister's memory is often romanticized and grandiose. If you were a participant in an event or conversation recorded in this book and you do not feel it happened exactly as I have conveyed it, then feel free to write your own book with your own version of the story. I'm a preacher. We sometimes have to sacrifice facts for truth. We have a biblical precedent.

X. Finally, I have coveted Hemingway's succinctness, Styron's honest vulnerability, Dillard's vision, Nouwen's heart, Moore's edgy humor, and Peart's poetic pace. I've also coveted the marketability of some ministers who have little to say but a large audience who is willing to listen. Hey, just being honest.

I'm inviting you to break Commandment 7. (Go ahead, join the ranks of the rest of us sinners.) If you are a minister, feel free to steal any line, idea, construct, or piece of content that you might find useful in these sermons. If you are not a minister—in other words, a normal person—then steal a moment each day and read. I will enjoy sharing the time with you.

ADVENT AND EPIPHANY

IT'S ALL IN THE TONE OF YOUR VOICE

1st Sunday of Advent
Isaiah 40:1–10

It's Advent! Jesus is coming! What does this mean for the guy and the gal who sit in the pew every Sunday? I guess it all depends on how you say it—the tone of your voice.

My mother was a master of shifts in vocal tone. You couldn't just listen to *what* she was saying; you had to pay close attention to *how* she was saying it. Case in point—the typical maternal phrase—"Just wait until your father gets home." These words were, at times, used to convey *threat*.

My grandmother gave the best Christmas presents of anyone I've ever known. Her presents were rarely expensive. Many of them were homemade, rarely costing anything. She would knit toboggans as an annual wintertime gift. One year she hand-tailored vests and chaps to accompany the toy cowboy guns and holsters my parents had purchased. I thought that outfit was the greatest gift under the tree.

One Christmas morning, Grandma's "buzz saws" appeared under tree. The homemade entertainment devices were delicately wrapped in old matchboxes; they were the Christmas morning toy of choice that year. My grandmother had played with this simple toy when she was a child. The noisy toy was constructed by looping a length of string though two holes on a large button. The two ends of the string were then tied together. With the button positioned in the middle of the looped string, by grasping each end of the loop in separate hands, we would swing the string in a "jump-rope" fashion, and the weight of the button would twist the string. Once well twisted, we repeatedly pulled and relaxed the ends of the string. The button would spin with the untwisting and re-twisting of the string, making a buzzing sound.

Of course, a toy with the name "buzz saw" was obviously created for the terrorizing of siblings. The three boys in our family—myself included—chased our sister around the yard with our buzz saws and eventually caught her. Buzzing our buttons closer and closer to her ears, it finally, sort of accidentally, happened. Three sets of buttons and strings became terribly twisted into her long blond hair. She screamed to Mom and Mom screamed at us. Mom screamed those words of threat that have echoed, at least once, in the ears of every child: "Just wait until your father gets home!"

Threat. That is the tone of Zephaniah when he ponders and proclaims the coming of the Lord. Zephaniah saw that day as a day of punishment, a day of the issuance of judgment. Zephaniah said that the day of the Lord is coming, and it is going to be a day of crying and wailing and darkness and war and wrath and distress and anguish. That is the day of the Lord.

It is the same picture that Jesus occasionally paints. In Matthew 25, we find a collection of parables about virgins who are not prepared, an employee who does not use his talents while he awaits his master's return, and a multitude of folk who do not care for a list of needy persons in their midst. Each of these parables culminates with the return of the master and the punishment of the unprepared and the unfaithful. Threat lies between the lines.

When Jesus came to earth the first time, he challenged and confronted people's priorities. When Jesus comes again, his second advent will be a time of judgment and punishment. Such is the threatening tone of the prophet when he says, "Wait until your father gets home."

Sometimes, however, a different tone inhabits this phrase. One afternoon the phone rang at 927 Maybry Street, Eudora, Arkansas.

My mom answered it. Halfway through the conversation, I knew the identity of the caller. We knew she was talking with our dad. Something exciting had happened. Her eyes lit up, her eyebrows rose and she bounced up and down. When she hung up the phone, she turned and said to us, "Wait until your dad gets home!" This was not a tone to which three rambunctious boys and their victimized sister had become accustomed. This was a completely different tone. This was the tone of *reward*.

The local grocery store had a lottery-style drawing every week. A chicken-wire barrel was filled with entry cards. Each week, the entry cards were mixed, a name was drawn, and a prize was given away. This drawing was televised on the local station at noon every Saturday. On one particular Saturday, the Dant family name was drawn from the chicken-wire barrel. When Dad got home, we learned our family had a won a vacation to Six Flags over Texas. There was much rejoicing. To an eight-year-old, this was better than having your name written in the Book of Life! Six Flags over Texas! Joy and reward are as much a part of Christ's coming as is the threat of punishment and judgment.

The older I get, however, the less motivated and moved I am by the threat of punishment or the promise of reward. It is a different tone to which I am drawn. It is the tone of Isaiah 40 when he proclaims comfort and hope to the struggling and hopeless. Isaiah's tone tells of a God who enters our worlds and our circumstances in order to lift up valleys, level mountains, and straighten paths. When Isaiah says, "Wait until your Father comes home," the words are infused with *assurance* and *help*.

The most expensive Christmas gift I remember receiving as a child was a gold-colored Spyder bike. The chopper-style handlebars and banana seat were all the rage. As young boys, we lived on our bicycles. And anyone who spends as much time on bicycles as we did knows that bicycles have flat tires and broken chains and loosened seats and handlebars and the ever-present need for a 9/16 wrench.

We would often find the wrench but also find we were not strong enough to loosen or tighten the needy nut or bolt. If we ran to our mom for assistance, she would always respond, "Wait until your father gets home." These were not words of reward or words of punishment. They were simply words that assured us of the advent of help.

"...And you shall call his name Emmanuel—God with us." God with us. Not just in the "sweet by and by" doling out reward and punishment, but with us right now. "God with us" in the person of Christ. God with us in the promised presence of Christ. God with us regardless of what we are going through.

Advent. It literally means to arrive or to come. It is a season to celebrate and prepare for the coming of Christ at Christmas, the coming of Christ into our hearts, and the second coming of Christ into the world. But what does all this mean to the guy and the gal who sit in the pew Sunday after Sunday? It all depends on how you say it. It's all in the tone of your voice.

PUT ANOTHER LEAF IN THE TABLE

2nd Sunday of Advent
Mark 1:1–8

Sometime after Thanksgiving, we would push the stepladder underneath the attic opening in the hallway of our home at 927 Maybry Street, Eudora, Arkansas. The rectangular hole in our hallway ceiling was covered with a painted, inset piece of plywood. From the top step of the rickety wooden ladder, the assigned climbers would hoist themselves into the attic and hand down all the Christmas necessities.

First would come the boxed silver Christmas tree—purchased from the Sears catalogue store many years before. Following the tinseled tree were boxes of ornaments and lights and bows and, of course, the electric candles that lit the front windows of our home. This regimen of retrieval was never complete, however, until my mother screamed from somewhere in the house, "Don't forget we have to put another leaf in the table." We would roll our eyes and then begin the search for the long piece of wood that was wedged somewhere between the dusty boxes and exposed rafters. We would hand it down through the ceiling hole, down the stepladder, and into the dining room. Wrestling the syrup-jelly-honey-stuck table in half, we settled the leaf in place and pushed the table together.

Normally one leaf in the table was plenty. Our family consisted of a mom and dad and four children. One leaf made seating for six fine, but we always had to add the second at Christmas time. That second leaf made room for company.

Uncle David's family always found their way to our table during the holiday season. Uncle David smelled like gasoline. He owned a filling station. I once asked him the difference between a filling station and a service station. He said, quite matter-of-factly, "We just fill you up. We don't clean your windshield or check your oil."

He only had two suits of clothes that I knew of. He had a pair of khaki Dickies shirts and pants and a pair of green Dickies pants and shirts. He was always in one of those two outfits. He enjoyed CB radios and harbored some strange beliefs. He believed that John F. Kennedy was still alive and residing on an island somewhere in the Bahamas. He also believed in alien abductions. The children in our household dreaded his visits. But our parents would sit us down, explain that everyone is a little different (our raised eyebrows prompted them to revise their speech to "Okay, a lot different"), and remind us that Uncle David was part of the family. So we put a second leaf in the table.

Then there was Aunt Ethel, and everyone has an Aunt Ethel. She was a dear lady who gave too much of herself away...far too much of herself. From the moment she walked into our home, she was hugging us and kissing us and pinching us on the cheeks. We endured her overly overt displays of affection because we loved her homemade cinnamon rolls.

Throwing the necessary ingredients onto our kitchen counter, she would frantically mix and knead and roll and sprinkle so that the melt-in-your-mouth sweet sensations would be ready by suppertime. We all hated the way she would lick her fingers while she was making them and then excitedly exclaim (as she jammed her wet fingers back into the dough), "These are really going to be good!" Whether giggling or gagging, our parents would quietly, inconspicuously remind us that Aunt Ethel was part of the family. So we put another leaf in the table.

And who could forget the DiPiatros. An old Army buddy of Dad's, Mr. DiPiatro and his family would travel from New England to Arkansas about once every three years to visit us. I barely knew them. I knew they were Yankees. I knew they were Catholics. I knew they had as many children as my family did, and when they came, we had to buy them all presents, and when my parents bought them presents, there was less money for the purchase of our presents—if you know what I mean. We were evicted from our bedrooms and forced to forage for floor space on which to sleep. A visit from the DiPiatros meant less gifts and less comfort, but our parents reminded us that they were family. Not blood relative, but family just the same. So we put another leaf in the table.

Every year we put another leaf in the table. We made room for people. People we had to hug. People we had to welcome. People we had to tolerate. People for whom we sacrificed because in some strange way, they were a part of our family.

You know how hard it is to put another leaf in the table. We drag that leaf out of the attic. Get on opposite sides of the dining table and pull and pull and pull. And the longer it's been since you put another leaf in the table, the harder it is to pull the table apart. You line up the rods with the holes and you finally push it back together, making room for a few more.

Putting another leaf in the table, I believe, is what the gospel—and maybe Christmas—is all about. Did you hear how Mark starts his gospel? "The beginning of the good news of Jesus Christ. As it is written, I am sending a messenger to you—put another leaf in the table. John the Baptist appeared proclaiming in the wilderness." Put another leaf in the table. All the people in the Judean countryside came to hear him. Put another leaf in the table. Everyone from the city of Jerusalem came to hear him. Put another leaf in the table.

Of course, it all started before John the Baptist. The angels came to Elizabeth before John was born and said, "You are going to have a child in your old age." Put another leaf in the table. The angels came to Mary and said, "A child will be born to you." Put another leaf in the table. The angel came to the shepherds and said, "I bring you good tidings of great joy which shall be to all people. A savior has been born!" Put another leaf in the table.

Jesus continued this welcoming tradition throughout his life. He called Levi, the tax collector, and the first thing Jesus did was eat at Levi's house. And Levi invited all of his friends to meet Jesus. Put another leaf in the table. Jesus met a Samaritan woman at the well, and she invited all the men of her city to come and meet Jesus. Put another leaf in the table. Jesus called prostitutes and publicans and Pharisees to follow him. He just kept calling and calling and calling and calling and welcoming and welcoming and welcoming. The gospel writers are constantly pulling another leaf out of the attic to accommodate Jesus' expanding family.

Now there were some who were horrified by Jesus' gracious welcoming of all these people—the tax collectors, Pharisees, publicans, prostitutes, saints, sinners. And today, there are those who cringe at the inclusion of persons at the table whose lifestyles, beliefs, behaviors, and backgrounds differ from what we consider normative. They would readily admit it is hard to put another leaf in the table...particularly if you haven't put one in for a long time.

I complained once about having to pull the leaf out of the attic and put it into our dining room table—but only once. I went into one of those youthful diatribes—a verbal essay expressing the discomforts that no one else seemed courageous enough (or arrogantly idiotic enough) to state. "We don't like it when Uncle David comes! He smells funny and he believes in aliens! And Aunt Ethel hugs us and kisses us and we are too old for that! And she licks her fingers and we're too sanitary for that. And for goodness sake, the DiPiatros aren't even kin to us! Why do we have to put a second leaf in the table?!"

My mom very quietly, very gently, placed her hand on my shoulder and walked me into the dining room. She took me to the edge of our dining room table, placed her hand on the one leaf that rested in the table year-round, and said, "We put this one here for you."

She was right. I was adopted when I was in the third grade. My younger brother was adopted too. Before the two of us came, that one round dining room table provided plenty of room for a family of four. Their older, biological children had never had to share a bedroom or sacrifice a measure of their Christmas bounty before I came. It was true. Before my adoption, they didn't need the first leaf in the table. They had to add a leaf for me. And with that realization, it wasn't so hard to stretch the table and make room for Uncle David and Aunt Ethel and all those other weird and wonderful people who made their way to our home during Christmas season.

This is the beginning of the gospel of Christ. As it is written, I am sending a messenger to you—put another leaf in the table. John the Baptist appeared proclaiming in the wilderness. Put another leaf in the table. All the people in the Judean countryside came to hear him. Put another leaf in the table. Everyone from the city of Jerusalem came to hear him. Put another leaf in the table.

I think the secret to having a wonderful Advent and Christmas season—or to just being a healthy church—is to add as many leaves to the table as possible. Invite a friend or neighbor to church. Put another leaf in the table. Welcome the guests who grace our presence during the Christmas Eve service and other special seasonal events. Put another leaf in the table. And if you are looking for a faith family—a church home—join us. We'll gladly put another leaf in the table.

NOT WHAT I EXPECTED

3rd Sunday of Advent
Matthew 11:2–11

You know "the look." A father says he wants a tie for Christmas. In his mind, he pictures a nice striped or paisley pattern to compliment perfectly his conservative gray, pin-striped suit. In his child's mind, the perfect tie sports the Tasmanian Devil...dressed in women's clothing...playing tennis. The father opens his gift on Christmas morning and the child's imagination has won out. It's that look. The look that is followed with fatherly accolades like, "How nice! This is exactly what I wanted. How did you know?" (It's a really interesting tie, but I do not wear it often.)

Dads aren't the only ones who fashion "the look." One of my daughters has informed me that all she wants for Christmas is a Jeep Grand Cherokee and a cell phone. On Christmas morning, when she awakens to Santa's stacked stash of socks and sweaters and maybe even a new Bible, she will produce "the look."

It's the same look we see on John the Baptist's face as he sits in his prison cell. In Matthew 11, it is painfully obvious that John the Baptist did not get what he wanted for Christmas. Whatever the Christ child was and whatever the Christ child became, it wasn't what John the Baptist had in mind. You remember John the Baptist's Christmas list don't you?

John told us what he wanted for Christmas. Eight chapters earlier, in Matthew 3, we did not see sugar plums dancing in John's dreams. Rather, he wanted an ax-wielding, fire-baptizing, wrathful winnower of chaff who would throw unrepentant tax collectors, Pharisees, prostitutes, and Romans into unquenchable fire! That's what John wanted for Christmas.

What John wanted—what John expected—was a Messiah who would condemn to hell those whom John felt deserved hell. And, of course, the Messiah would reward those—like John—who deserved grace. So it's not hard to imagine "the look" on John's face as he sat in prison. This was not what he had expected.

It's the same look that swept across the older brother's face when the prodigal child came home and received a multitude of gifts from his dad: a ring, a robe, sandals, and a party. I can easily imagine the thoughts running through the older brother's head: "Uh, Dad, if you are making a list and checking it twice in order to find out who's been naughty and who's been nice, then you've got it all wrong. I deserve the ring and robe and sandals. He deserves the bag of coal."

You know the look. You know the thoughts. We've all had that look on our faces at one time or another. Those thoughts have run through most of our minds—probably more than once.

I regret some of the earliest sermons of my preaching career. I spent precious time, in front of precious people, with "the look" on my face, those thoughts in my head, and yes, the words on my lips. I manipulated and coerced people with sermons designed to invoke guilt and shame and fear rather than celebrate the enormous grace of God. This really said more about me than it did the people in the pew or the God that's in heaven. I lived with a spiritual schizophrenia of sorts, like many of you do. I was thankful that God loved me despite "my sins," but I was certain God would punish "them" because of their sins. When I sinned, God loved and forgave me. When "they" sinned, God angrily demanded justice. I was limiting God's grace. Again, it said a lot about me and my prejudices.

I think John the Baptist was shocked at the gracefulness of the gospel. I think he was taken aback by the stark contrast between his words and the words of Jesus. And yet, somewhere deep inside of John, he must have known—just like I knew. After all, in Matthew 3, when John finishes his wish list of axes and winnowing forks and fire, he looks up and sees Jesus. And before he can think, before he can filter his words through the religiosity of his normal rhetoric, he exclaims, "Behold the Lamb of God who takes away the sins of the world!" Not just his own sins. Not just the repented sins of soldiers and tax collectors. But the sins of the world.

This was not what John wanted or expected. And as he sits alone in prison, you can see "the look" on his face. You can hear it in his questions. Are you really the one or should we look for another?

Jesus told John who he was. Jesus sent John's disciple back to him with a message. The blind are receiving sight. The lame are walking. Lepers are being touched and healed. The ears of the deaf are being opened. The graves are being opened! The poor are having opportunities opened to them!

But there was no winnowing fork in his hand. In fact, when presented with an adulterous woman—caught in the act—he didn't even pick up a stone. And there was no wrath in his voice. In fact, with his dying breath, he would welcome a thief into paradise and pray forgiveness upon the very crowd John had damned.

Jesus brought the free gifts of forgiveness and eternal life into the world. Deep down, John knew it. But when visions of axes and winnowing forks are dancing in your head, grace is often hard to see and accept and proclaim.

In Philip Gulley and James Mulholland's wonderful book, *If Grace Is True: Why God Will Save Every Person*, they relay this story:

When my son was five, we were preparing to attend some function where we all needed to be well dressed. We gave my son a bath and put on his nicest clothes, and then my wife and I began to prepare ourselves. Our son, bored and impatient, asked to go outside and play. We finally gave in but made it clear he was not to get dirty. He promised to be good.

About five minutes after he went outside, our doorbell rang. Standing at our doorstep was our neighbor and a little boy with mud caked from the top of his head to the tip of his toe. He had tried to jump over a mud puddle and failed. Our neighbor asked, "Is this your son?"

For a moment I thought about saying no. But grace won out. I took him by the hand and led him upstairs to his second bath. I claimed him and cleaned him. His filthy condition did not change our relationship. Indeed, it only emphasized how much he needed me.[1]

Merry Christmas. I'm not sure what you're expecting to receive this year, but if that kind of grace is more than you ever dreamed you would receive, then Merry Christmas.

---

[1] Philip Gulley and James Mulholland, *If Grace Is True: Why God Will Save Every Person* (New York: HarperCollins Publishers, Inc., 2003) 72–73.

CHRISTMAS RESPONSES

4th Sunday of Advent
Matthew 1:18–25

My favorite Christmas decoration is not really a decoration at all. It is a photo album we place on our living room coffee table for the duration of December. The album chronicles our children's responses to Christmas over the last eighteen years. There is one picture from each year.

There are early pictures of our children on Santa's lap and later pictures of our children standing in front of the Christmas tree. It is interesting to flip through the years and see how their responses to Christmas have evolved and changed.

Of course, there is baby's first Christmas, eight months old, sitting on Santa's lap, oblivious to seasonal bliss, mouth half open, eyes in a daze. The early preschool pictures capture curious faces looking intently at the jolly old elf—not quite certain who this fellow is. Later preschool snapshots prompt memories of the screaming or crying—old enough to fear the fur-faced fellow. By elementary school, their Christmas eyes are filled with excitement. The dullness and distress of prior years have passed with the understanding of "making a list." And then come the teenage years—arms folded, head tilted, standing in front of the Christmas tree with that look on their face that says, "Hurry up with the family-tradition thing. I've got friends to meet at the mall." Eighteen years of Christmas responses in one photo album.

In Matthew, chapter 1, we get three different responses to the Christmas miracle in just a few verses. It says the birth of Jesus happened this way. It took place when Mary, who had been engaged to Joseph, but before they lived together, found out she was pregnant. Joseph, was a righteous man. While he couldn't find it in himself to love and raise the child, he certainly didn't want to expose her publicly. He assumed the worst, I'm sure. But he refused to allow "the worst" to dictate his actions and reactions.

There are some folk who see the bad and the negative in everything. Christmas is no different for them. They live life in the realm of negativity and critique. They believe there is a dreadful truth about this season that must be told. *They feel a need to expose Christmas.*

My childhood memories are peppered with recollections of certain loud people talking about the pagan roots of Christmas. They vigorously asserted that December 25 was historically a day when the ancients celebrated the sun. They further argued that Christmas trees were idols and the placing of gifts beneath their decorated boughs were tantamount to idol worship. "It's a pagan holiday!" they screamed. "I'm exposing Christmas for what it truly is!"

Other voices are less concerned with the season's pagan roots and more concerned with its modern commercialization. These individuals provide us with salient sermons and numerous examples of "the marketing of the holiday." They pontificate with an air of arrogant insight, "It's just one big billion-dollar racket that keeps the economy rolling, the toy stores open, minimum wage earners employed, and the postal service in business." And I guess they're right. Of course, this is not some unique insight; we all know it. The season is quite commercialized. But what moves a person to be the whistle blower on Kris Kringle? Why does this need to be exposed?

Joseph, a righteous man, chose not to expose Mary. Joseph responded to the Christmas miracle with a question mark in his mind, I'm sure. But he refused the first option of response. He had no desire to expose Mary. He had no desire to expose her to the criticism of her peers or to the whispers of the community or the consequences of the law—stoning. Joseph refused this first response to Christmas—exposing the negative.

Have you finished your commercialized Christmas shopping for this pagan holiday yet? Here's a suggestion. One of the greatest gifts you can give this Christmas season will cost you very little. Look for and make note of the good in people rather than the bad. Don't take delight in exposing people's flaws, but take every opportunity to encourage and to nurture what is good in people. The first response to Christmas we encounter in this text is to expose it for what it really is. I am glad Joseph avoids this response and moves on to the second.

Unwilling to expose Mary to public disgrace, Joseph planned to *dismiss her quietly.* Juxtaposed to exposure, this seems merciful enough. Set her aside. Put her away. Act as if the friendship, the engagement, and the love had never existed. Just pretend it never happened. Just pretend she doesn't exist. Get on with your life.

Leo Buscaglia, a popular psychologist in the 1970s, said the opposite of love is not hate. When we hate someone we, give them energy, time, and attention. The opposite, according to Buscaglia, is to ignore them—to dismiss them quietly.

It's not easy to dismiss or ignore Christmas. After all, there are lights down every street, manger scenes on every corner, Christmas trees in every window, and music on every loud speaker that we pass. But for many, life has been so stressful and so painful and so bleak that they are tempted to respond to Christmas by taking the joy and the hope and the peace of the season and dismissing it quietly. They are trying their best to get through December 25...and move on.

Again, in case you have not finished your Christmas shopping, here's another wonderful gift you could give this season that will cost you very little. Give someone your attention and your presence. The opposite of love is to be ignored ,and there are a lot of people ignored by humanity and whp feel ignored by God during this season.

During our church's Wednesday night supper hour, I am often amazed at my church members' concern for my nutritional needs. When I am meandering around the tables, greeting each of them, many of them ask the same questions over and over: "When are you going to eat? Are you going to eat? Did you know you could dry up and blow away if you don't eat?"

I promise that I do eat. I make my rounds to every table, then go back to my table and eat. The proof? I haven't dried up and blown away. It is important for me, on Wednesday evenings, to greet each of my church members—at every table. It is my way of saying that they are not ignored. They are loved.

Last week I walked into a room at a local nursing home. "Merry Christmas!" I exclaimed as I stepped through the door. The dear soul lived there, slept there, and daydreamed there. She looked at me and began to cry.

Wiping her tears with a crumpled tissue, she said, "Thank you so much for coming by."

A lot of people feel ignored. Last Tuesday, one of my fellow parishioners came by my office after lunch. We both expected the conversation to last for about five minutes. An hour and a half later, we finished our conversation. My friend got up to leave, turned to me, and said, "This was so good. I'm glad we didn't just pass in the hallway, say hello, settle our business, and leave. It's been good to sit down and talk."

Both responses, in Matthew 1:19, fall short of my expectations for this holiday season. Expose her. Dismiss her. Neither feels comfortable. I'm glad there is at least one other response in the story.

When Joseph had resolved to do all this, an angel of the Lord appeared to him in a dream and told him to take Mary as his wife. When Joseph awoke from his sleep, he did as the angel of the Lord commanded him. He took her to be his wife. *He took her, he embraced her, and he welcomed her into his life.* This is the final, most appropriate response to Christmas.

Joseph went beyond the requirements and the expectations of the law. He rejected the idea of an eye for an eye and a tooth for a tooth. He didn't claim his legal rights. He didn't dismiss her quietly. He went beyond the law and welcomed her into his life. Before grace ever became part of Christian theology, Joseph was already allowing grace to guide his decisions. He took her. He embraced her. He welcomed her into his life.

I ran into our local rabbi this past Thursday in the grocery store. We passed each other on the cereal aisle. I said, "Happy Hanukkah, Rabbi," and he quickly responded, "Merry Christmas, Jim." We stopped and chatted.

In the course of our conversation, he asked, "What are you preaching about on Christmas Eve?"

"I'm pretty sure I'm going to be talking about the birth of Jesus," I sarcastically responded. We both laughed.

The rabbi told me he had been working on his Christmas Eve sermon. I laughed, assuming he was kidding. The mischievous look in his eyes, however, indicated he was not jesting.

"You realize," he said, "that Christmas Eve falls on the Sabbath this year."

He was right. Christmas Eve was on Friday night.

He told me he had decided to preach a Christmas sermon this year. After asking him what he planned to say, he told me he was going to share the traditional Christmas story from Luke 2. He planned to tell his congregation that this is the day Christians welcome God into their world—a child named Emmanuel, God with us.

"Then," he said, "I'm going to tell my people about the miracle you miss. Christmas isn't about welcoming God to our world; it's about God welcoming us to his world. God's world is a world where anything is possible—stars, miraculous births, angels—we Jews have experienced these phenomena for years! God's world is a world that welcomes wealthy kings and impoverished shepherds. God's world is simple and holy. God has come to our world many, many times. Bethlehem was God's invitation for you to come to his. The teachings of Jesus, as I understand them, are God's invitation for you to come to his world—his kingdom."

I said, "Happy Hanukkah."

He said, "Merry Christmas."

We went our separate ways.

I was loading my groceries into the trunk of the car. It really did make sense. The miracle of Christmas is not that we can welcome Christ into our world; the real miracle is that God welcomes us, all of us, into his world. This is the best and truest response to Christmas. This is the response God models. Take her. Embrace her. Welcome her into your life.

Joseph enjoyed, loved, and welcomed Mary. Parishioners, enjoy, love, and welcome Christmas. For God enjoys, loves, and welcomes us.

An Atlanta Rhythm Section Christmas

Christmas Eve, December 24, 2005
Luke 2:1–20

I like music. Christmas would not be complete without certain songs in the background: Karen Carpenter's deep rich voice singing "Merry Christmas Darling," Nat King Cole's smooth reminder that chestnuts are roasting on an open fire, Bing Crosby crooning "White Christmas," and yes, even Alvin and the Chipmunks begging, "Christmas Don't Be Late."

I was born in Mississippi. For me, Christmas isn't Christmas without Elvis's Christmas album. No one particular song; you have to listen to the whole album multiple times! "Blue Christmas," "White Christmas," "Santa Bring My Baby Back to Me," "It's Christmas Time Pretty Baby." I need every last groove of the old black vinyl to be needled. But hey, that's just me.

And maybe it's just me, but certain artists—certain Christmas albums—I don't get. For instance, Jimmy Buffet's *Christmas Island*. Don't get me wrong. I like Jimmy Buffet. I love rolling the windows down, middle of the summer, cruising the coastal highway of Florida's panhandle listening to "Margaritaville." There's nothing better. But *Christmas Island*? I don't get it.

I own a copy of the Star Wars Christmas album titled *Christmas in the Stars*. It includes that classic Christmas hit, "What Do You Get a Wookie for Christmas?" Who writes this stuff? Like I said, I own it…I just don't get it.

And I know I'm tampering with some "near classics" now, but how am I supposed to feel about Christmas albums by Kenny G.,

Barbara Streisand, and Barry Manilow? Aren't they Jewish? *Christmas* albums? There's no one more in tune with their Jewish roots than me, but I still don't get it!

On the other hand, some artists—some songs—*should* be considered Christmas worthy and yet are never included on Christmas albums. They never make the Muzak in the mall and they never make the radio playlist on Christmas Eve. Songs like "I'm Not Gonna Let It Bother Me Tonight" recorded by the Atlanta Rhythm Section. Do you remember the words?

> I picked up the paper this morning, and read all the daily blues.
> The world is one big tragedy, I wonder what I can do...
> About all the pain and injustice, about all of the sorrow,
> We're living in a danger zone, the world could end tomorrow.
>
> But I'm not gonna let it bother me tonight.
> I'm not gonna let it bother me tonight.
> The world is in an uproar and I see no end in sight.
> But I won't let it bother me tonight.
>
> Life on the streets is a jungle, a struggle to keep up the pace.
> I just can't beat that old dog-eat-dog, the rats keep winning the rat race.
>
> But I'm not gonna let it bother me tonight.
> I'm not gonna let it bother me tonight.
> The world is an uproar and I can see no end in sight,
> But I will not let it bother me tonight.

And therein lies a part of the meaning and the beauty of Christmas.

In Luke 2, the world is in an uproar. Caesar Augustus had called for a census, planning to increase taxes. Mary was miraculously pregnant but not married. (Miraculous in her mind...scandalous in everyone else's mind.) The streets were filled with families and donkeys. The inns were filled with travelers. The stable was filled with animals. The air was filled with rumors about the murderous jealousy of Herod. Men's dreams were filled with warnings. The evening hours were filled with visiting shepherds. (Just what every mother wants right after delivery.)

The world was in an uproar. Interestingly enough, our mental images of that first Christmas are always images filled with peace. With all the turmoil surrounding the holy family, they seem focused on the gift of the Christ child. Nothing else matters, at least for that moment.

In 1865, the world was in an uproar. At least William Dix's world was in an uproar. At the age of twenty-nine, he had contracted a sudden and serious illness. This prolonged illness led to a deep, dark, clinical depression. Unable to crawl out of bed for days, finally—at the encouragement of a friend—he picked up a pen and began to journal his feelings. After pages of pain, complaint, and lament, the pages began to reverberate with prayer. They were hard, questioning prayers at first. Soon, however, the rancid rigor gave way to reflection.

Amid his own suffering, he began to reflect upon the nature of Christ. He pondered the irony of Christ's sovereignty and suffering. In his journal, he thoughtfully juxtaposed the "Bread of Life" with being hungry. He struggled with the "Living Water" dying thirsty. He made entries concerning Jesus' weariness, his garden prayers of anguish, and his pitiful death. Dix, out of his own struggles, decided to follow in the painfully productive footsteps of his Lord. It was Dix who penned these words:

What child is this who laid to rest
On Mary's lap is sleeping?
Whom angels greet with anthem sweet
While shepherds watch are keeping.
This, this is Christ the King
Whom shepherds guard and angels sing.
Haste, haste to bring him laud—the babe, the son of Mary.

William Dix's world was in an uproar, and he saw no end in sight. But the one day, the one event that captured his attention and brought some solace to his soul, was Christmas.

Tonight, some of our worlds are in an uproar. But I'm not gonna let it bother me tonight.

Now I know what you are thinking. You think I'm just avoiding reality. You think I'm refusing to meet life head on, maybe even living in denial. I hear your concerns. I'm not interested in "living" in denial, however. I know that constantly pushing the realities of life aside is not healthy. But I also know that denial ain't so bad every once in a while. So I'm not gonna let it bother me tonight...because it's Christmas.

In Luke 2, two young parents are broke and tired. They had the weight of the government on their backs and a newborn baby in their arms. There was no room for them in the inn, but seemingly plenty of room for a family, animals, and a host of visiting shepherds in the barn. But they didn't let it bother them on that night...because it was Christmas.

In 1865, a twenty-nine-year-old man was too sick—physically and mentally—to slip from beneath his bed sheets and face the light of a new day. The darkness of an uncertain future loomed before him. But he didn't let him bother him, at least for one moment, while he pondered Christmas.

This Christmas Eve, we are a church full of folk whose world is in an uproar. We are living in a world that is pained by war, fraught with disease, riddled with crime, buried in debt, and plagued by terrorists. What's more, our personal worlds are in an uproar. We are struggling with the absence and loss of family and friends. We are struggling to care for children and parents. We are working our way through broken promises and marriages. We are hoping to make ends meet and habits cease, and the list goes on and on and on. But, but...

> I'm not gonna let it bother me tonight.
> I'm not gonna let it bother me tonight.
> The world is in an uproar and I see no end in sight.
> But I'm not gonna let it bother me tonight.

I'm going to receive and celebrate God's greatest gift to humankind. I am going to trust that gift will make a difference in all my tomorrows. I'm not gonna let it bother me tonight...because it's Christmas. What a perfect Christmas song.

FISH BAIT, AVON, AND AUTO PARTS

Sunday after Christmas
Luke 2:22–35

There is a little store that sits on a highway on the edge of the south Georgia metropolis of Nichols. In front of this store, on the highway, there is a painted sign that reads, "Fish Bait, Avon, and Auto Parts." If you pull into the gravel parking lot as I did on one particular day because I was thirsty and wanted a Dr. Pepper, you will also see a smaller sign affixed to the door that says, "If we ain't got it, you don't need it." I needed a Dr. Pepper for refreshment and renewal for the rest of my day's journey, and they had one. It was ice cold in a bottle, which is the best kind. As I drank my Dr. Pepper and browsed around the little store, I realized that over time they had come to anticipate the needs and wants of the people who lived in that little community. They even provided some of the desires of occasional passersby who were just driving through Nichols.

In Luke, chapter 2, Joseph, Mary, and the baby Jesus stop at the temple. They find at this one venue what they need to renew and restore and refresh them for the long journey ahead. While at the temple, *Mary and Joseph found the power of a ritual.* In verse 22, they bring Jesus to the temple to dedicate him as was their custom and their law. According to the book of Exodus, every firstborn male child was to be brought to the temple and dedicated as a reminder of God's goodness in the deliverance in Egypt and a reminder of their hope for the future. That's the power of a ritual.

Tom followed me as a pastor at Mount Olivet Baptist Church in Tatum Springs, Kentucky. During his first year as pastor there, he telephoned me regarding a problem. "A baby was recently born to one of our church families," he said, "and the parents want the child dedicated. They said I was supposed to carry the baby up and down the aisle of the church and talk to it! I told the mother that I wasn't carrying any baby up and down the aisle of the church. I wasn't comfortable with that. She started crying. Now, exactly how do you do this dedication thing?" That's the power of a ritual.

I enjoy e-mail correspondence with some former members who moved out of town recently. In one of the e-mails, they told me that they have been looking for a new church and, I quote, "and just when you think you are tired of the doxology, you can't find a church that sings it…and we miss it." The power of a ritual.

A college student who was attending our church last week shook my hand as he was leaving the sanctuary. I told the young man that I was glad to have him there. He said, "I was glad to be here." He said, "You know what? I haven't sung 'Footsteps of Jesus' since I was a kid." The power of a ritual.

Many Baptist churches have reduced the celebration of communion to once a quarter or once a year. Some churches have eliminated hymns and doxologies and readings and responses and wouldn't even think of singing Handel's *Messiah* at Christmas. That's okay, I guess. But I'm glad that we intentionally choose to be different, to proudly embrace the rituals of our faith and believe that they really do renew, refresh, and nurture us week after week after week. Mary and Joseph went to the temple and found the power of ritual.

They also found there the power of a gift. And so, according to the law, they brought their sacrifice and offered it on behalf of the baby Jesus—two turtledoves and two pigeons. At every baby dedication, we give a Bible. In fact, over the years at Highland Hills, our children receive several gifts—a Bible at their dedication, a certificate at their baptism, a first communion cup at their first communion, another Bible when they enter first grade, another Bible when they enter the youth group, and many gifts from us when they graduate from high school. The reason we do this is because we believe that significant gifts bestowed on children will impact and influence their lives.

An old Chinese proverb says, "A child's life is like a piece of paper on which every person leaves a mark." Tristen lives down the street from me. Tristen's parents asked me if I would bring him home from church a few weeks ago, so he hopped in the car and we headed to Craddock Way where we both live. I turned the radio on, and all of a sudden we heard "Sweet Home Alabama" Tristen excitedly asked, "Would you turn that up? That's my favorite song."

"Tristen," I curiously asked, "do you know the name of that song?"

"Sweet Home Alabama," he said with a confident smile.

"That's right."

We drove another 100 yards or so, and Tristen spoke again. "Mr. Jim, would you pull over and buy me a Yoo-hoo?"

"A what?" I asked.

"A Yoo-hoo."

"Why do you need a Yoo-hoo?"

"I like to drink Yoo-hoos while I listen to this song."

This past Sunday night, the Atlanta Braves were playing their final game against the Chicago Cubs, and I thought about Tristen. I figured, anybody that drinks one Yoo-hoo while listening to Lynard Skynard probably drinks a six-pack while watching the Atlanta Braves. So I stopped and picked up a six-pack of Yoo-hoos, ice cold in the bottles. I took them to Tristen's house. He was ecstatic to receive them. I was happier to give them. I was the one who received the real joy that night by handing him those Yoo-hoos. Seeing his eyes light up and hearing him say, "Thank you, Mr. Jim," I knew that I had left a mark on his sheet of paper. He may never remember a sermon I preach, but he will never forget the Yoo-hoos.

In verse 24, the gifts that are given are not gifts given to Jesus, the baby; they are gifts given on his behalf. The kinds of gifts that teach us that we receive the greatest joy when we are the givers, not the receivers. I can't think of a better time than when we dedicate a child to say before God that we are going to give the best of our time and the best of our talents and the best of our energies and the best of our resources to make sure that child is nurtured toward faith in Christ. The power of a gift.

In Luke, chapter 2, *Mary and Joseph and Jesus also encounter the power of a word.* The text says Simon took the child and prayed, saying, "God, you have finally let your promises come true in my life and you let your promises come true for the world." Then it says he blessed them. Simon blessed the family.

Our baby dedications have become a lot like stock car races. That's right. A good friend finally confessed to me that he only watches stock car races for the wrecks. I think after several dedications, I feel the only reason some of you came today was to see if the baby would cry! After every dedication, people come to me and say, "We keep waiting for one to cry." There are a lot of theories about why the babies don't cry. One theory is that they are looking at the chandeliers as I walk. One theory is that it's the way I pat the baby and rock and sway. Another theory is that I have chloroform on the stole that I wear on Baby Dedication Day! The most dominant theory I hear, however, is that it's the voice. When I am talking to the baby, well, to put it into the words of one member, "You know, those baby dedications are just like your sermons—I listen to them and go right to sleep." Maybe it's the voice; I don't know. The power of a word.

The last thing I say to the child before I give that child back to the parents is always, "God bless you, _____." Simon blessed them. What does that mean? When one person invokes God's blessings upon another person, it at least means this: God is going to be with you for the rest of the journey, and since I'm speaking the blessing, I'm going to be with you for the rest of the journey also.

I had lunch with my friend, Rob, several weeks ago. During the course of that luncheon, he said, "Jim, you have been here seven years now, and I know there are other churches where you might like to work. I want to know how long you are going to be at the church."

I looked at Rob and said, "My first Sunday at Highland Hills was Father's Day. We dedicated your oldest child that morning. Rob, to be perfectly honest, nothing would make me happier than to stay long enough to baptize her, congratulate her on her graduation from high school, and even pronounce blessings upon her marriage. When I dedicated your child, I said 'God bless you, Miller,' which means, God be with you and I'm with you too...for the journey. Not only during the good times, but also during those hard times of broken bones and broken hearts.

Fish Bait, Avon, and Auto Parts. If we don't have it, you don't need it. The church is not a perfect place. We don't do everything right. But over the years, we have learned to anticipate the needs of people. We have found that in their lives, ritual and gift and word have the power to renew and refresh and strengthen.

TURN ON THE STAR

Epiphany Sunday
Matthew 2:1–12

Allow me tell you a true story from the vivid mind and memory of Robert Fulghum. He recalls that he had never seen a live donkey ridden through a church sanctuary, but on one particular Christmas, it seemed a fine thing to do. The great day came and everybody arrived at the church for the Christmas pageant. It wasn't all that bad, really. The choir got through its first big number almost on key and in unison. The star of Bethlehem was lit over the manger, and then the time came for the entrance of Joseph and Mary. It was the live donkey that proved their undoing.

The donkey made two hesitant steps into the sanctuary, took a look at the whole scene, and seized up—locked his legs well beyond rigor mortis—and the whole procession ground to a halt. Now there are some things you might consider doing to a donkey in private to get it to move, but there is a limit to what you can do to a donkey in church on Sunday in front of the women and children. Even the wicked kicking on the part of the Virgin Mary had no effect, so the chairman of the board of deacons, who was seated in the front row dressed in his Sunday finest, rose to the rescue.

The floor of the sanctuary was polished cement, so with another man pulling and the chairman of the deacons pushing at the rigid beast, they were able slowly to slide the donkey across the floor. With this kind of progress being made, the choir director turned back on the tape recorder, which blared forth a mighty chorus from the Mormon Tabernacle Choir. Just as the donkey and his pushers reached mid-church, the tape recorder blew a fuse and there was a sudden silence. In that silence, an exasperated voice was heard from the rear of the donkey saying, "You better move your blankity blankity blankity blank!" followed immediately by the voice of the chairman of the deacons' wife from the back of church saying, "Leon, shut your filthy mouth!" It has been several years since they have had another Christmas pageant. But the memory of that laughter lives on.

I love it when church programs go bad and you do too; don't judge me too harshly. I have watched the audience for years in our amphitheatre during the live nativity productions. They want something to go wrong. They want some excitement. They want that poor donkey Poncho to do something, whether it's bray when the angel comes out, try to fling the baby Jesus out of the manger, or maybe force Mary to feed him a little bit so that he will stay out of the stable. We all like it when church programs go bad.

My favorite church program gone bad was at Glenwood Hills Methodist Church. Our youth group had been invited to watch their youth group's Christmas pageant. Mary and Joseph and the bathrobe-bedecked shepherds all made their way to their assigned places. The lights were dimmed to near darkness. An offstage narrator read from Matthew 2 about the entrance of the Magi. Then, all of a sudden, we heard a loud crash! Gold and frankincense and myrrh and Magi seemed to be tumbling everywhere in the middle of the darkness. Finally, when all the noise subsided, a small voice was heard from the stage area saying, "Will someone please turn on the star?" At that point, the light technician turned on the star, which was supposed to have illuminated a way for the wise men to come. Obviously, in the darkness, one wise man had stepped on the front of his robe coming up the steps. He had tripped, causing everyone else to trip over him, and the light only illuminated regal carnage. Will somebody please turn on the star?

To modern audiences, the Magi are just good comedy. When you turn on the star at the Christmas pageant, the wise men come in. They are usually three adults wearing barely better-than-average bathrobe costumes that add a dash of color and a bit of the exotic to the otherwise fairly rustic nature of the whole manger scene. To modern audiences, when you turn on the star to let the Magi enter, we all know that it is the comedic climactic conclusion to the Christmas pageant—the wise men have come.

To Matthew's audience, the Magi were not good comedy; they were scandal. The wise men were probably anything but wise to Matthew's audience. In fact, they were almost certainly not kings, even though our hymns tend to support that. The Greek word used for Magi is the ancient word for magician, stargazer, and astrologer, or one who tries to interpret present and future events based on how the stars are aligned. These men were the Jeane Dixons of the ancient world—1–800-Dial Sister Cleo! The Old Testament condemns Magi and calls them idolatrous deceivers. One rabbi writing before the birth of Jesus said that anyone who learns from a Magi deserves death. Added to all that, to Matthew's audience, the Magi were those bumblers who tipped Herod off about the birth of Jesus. If these Magi had never questioned Herod, the bloody massacre of the innocents would have never occurred. To Matthew's audience, when the star is turned on and the Magi enter, it is a scandal. It would have certainly prompted the question, "How can people like that be welcomed next to the Messiah?"

Matthew has been flirting with this question since the beginning of his gospel. I have been doing a study of the Gospels at a local retirement home on Monday afternoons. A couple of weeks ago, the group was instructed to read the book of Matthew and come with their observations and questions. When the time for our study began, I asked, "Does anyone have any observations from your reading?"

One of the residents raised his hand and said, "That was the strangest genealogy that I have ever read."

"Excuse me?"

"I am assuming," he continued, "that this is supposed to be a Jewish genealogy. But it didn't fit the pattern I had assumed it would follow."

With a curious eyebrow raised, I asked him what he meant.

"There are women in the genealogy," he said. "There are also gentiles and a few scandalous folk. I didn't think women and gentiles and scoundrels were supposed to be included in a formal Jewish genealogy."

My student received his genealogical education from a very astute Sunday school teacher. And his observation was correct. The genealogy and the Magi are both part of Matthew's sneak preview of the reach of Jesus' ministry...the reach of the gospel.

The same Christ that drew Magi to the manger in Matthew's gospel is going to be the same Christ that has the magnetic appeal to draw Samaritans, adulteresses, prostitutes, greasy tax collectors, Roman soldiers, and ostracized lepers. In fact, Matthew's view seems to be that when we turn on the star, there is no telling who is going to show up. For Matthew's audience, it's a scandal. With that in mind, when you turn on the star, there is no telling who is going to turn up.

For the church, the Magi are a challenge. When we turn on our star, when we let our light shine before men, there is no telling who is going to show up. The challenge for the church becomes how open the church will be. This is the Sunday of Epiphany. The word "epiphany" means the appearing or the appearance. It's a Sunday when we celebrate the appearance of the Magi. It is also a Sunday for congregations to ponder a few questions. Questions like "What kind of church will we be this year?", "How open will our front doors be this year?" "How open will our hearts be this year?", "When somebody from the outside comes inside, what are they going to sense and feel and experience?"

Today our manger scene is finally complete, and that hodgepodge of shepherds and animals and angels and parents and infants and Magi and all those wildly diverse people are all gathered around Christ under one little roof. It reminds us of the reality of what the church is supposed to be. A hodgepodge of all different kinds of people gathered together around Christ under one roof—under his star. Because, when you turn on the star, there's no way to predict who will show up. That's the challenge for the church.

MANLY MEN

Men's Day
Mark 6:14–29

This is Men's Day. I do feel, however, that I should be completely honest with you. So I will. You realize that we all begin as females. From the moment of conception, our developing brains and our developing bodies are all females. It is only later in fetal development that particular hormones kick in and prompt some of us to become males. Men—basically and biologically—are modified females. Comedian George Carlin has his own take on this phenomenon. He claims that while we all began as females, some of us have "evolved to the heights of maleness." In all fairness, one of my more militant feminist friends has retorted, "I looked at the same data and concluded that some fetuses mutate into maleness."

These feminine beginnings have probably prompted some men to feel as if they must prove their masculinity. Many become slaves to this internal force—this internal drive—that scientists have called testosterone. It's not hard to spot them. These hormonally driven gentlemen tend to gather. They create subcultures, and these subcultures tend to be obsessed with things like wheels and weapons and whiskey and women and winning. In fact, the chemical formula for testosterone—if you didn't know it already—is equal parts of gasoline, gunpowder, adrenaline, and alcohol. Put them all together and you've got testosterone.

Realizing this was Men's Day, one of our parishioners sent me an e-mail. She felt I might like to use its contents in my sermon. I will oblige. Her e-mail stated that the Pentagon has put together an elite fighting force of 5,000 Southern men. They have flown them over Iraq and dropped them into enemy territory. Before deployment, this Southern fighting force was given limited information and instruction. They were told hunting season is open on Iraqis; there is no limit; they taste like chicken; they don't like beer, country music, or Jesus; and they are solely responsible for the death of Dale Earnhardt. At the bottom of the e-mail—in fine print and parentheses—it said "The war should be over by Friday." That's testosterone.

This whole testosterone thing seems to be Herod's problem. Almost the whole of Mark 6 records the one highlight in Herod's life. In fact, this narrative story is the longest story in the gospel of Mark that is not about Jesus. It is about Herod. And the sad thing is, his fifteen minutes in the limelight are wasted on his overabundance of testosterone. I know First Timothy says the love of money is the root of all evil, but when you read about Herod in Mark 6, you have got to start thinking it might be testosterone. Now, for all of you biblical scholars who love to delve into the details, you need to know this is not the Herod who killed all of Bethlehem's babies. That was Herod the Great. Of course, his ridiculous display of violence might well be attributed to the competitive side effects of testosterone. He wanted to be the only, the best, the biggest king.

The Herod of Mark 6 is also not the Herod Agrippa of Acts 12—the ruler who executed John the brother of James. Alas, testosterone.

Our Herod is Herod Antipas. His acts of notorious notoriety certainly rival his namesakes. Everything we know about Herod Antipas points toward a sinful self-indulgent man suffering from the effects of testosterone. What do we know about him? He had an affair with his brother's wife and ended up marrying her—testosterone. He threw a party for himself—testosterone. Had his stepdaughter come and dance for the men—testosterone. (And by the way, these seductive dances usually took place in a private chamber where only men and dancers were allowed. I have no idea what all went on in there, but I'm guessing it had something to do with…yep…testosterone.) They were probably drunk—testosterone. They were all lustfully pleased by what they saw—testosterone. Herod stands up at the end of the party and proudly offers his dancing diva, "I'll buy you anything you want, up to half my kingdom." He pulls out his platinum MasterCard just to prove he can afford it—testosterone.

You have heard how all Alabama men die, haven't you? Their last four words are always, "Hey man, watch this!" That is exactly what Herod said. "Hey man, watch this. I bet you I can get my brother's wife to look at me. And then I'll throw a party and then I'll get my stepdaughter to dance for us and then I'll give her anything she wants!" Testosterone, testosterone, testosterone. And the result of all this? The death of an innocent prophet. The one man in the whole story who is giving good attention to God's law, the one man who—even if it means he has to go to prison—is going to speak and do what is right. That man dies. The drunk always seem to survive the accident. The innocent always seem to die—testosterone.

At the other end of the male spectrum, woven into this raucous story, there are some obscure characters whose lives are not primarily driven by testosterone. Rather, their lives are driven by their testimonies—their personal faith testimonies. In contrast to Herod's self-indulgence, the disciples of Jesus move into the world with no bread and no bag and nothing in their pockets—empty handed. As meek as they may appear, they have been endowed with the power to preach repentance, cast out demons, and cure the people. In contrast to Herod's dismissal of God's law, there is John the Baptist who speaks and lives the truth even if it means imprisonment—even if the means his head ends up on a platter. In contrast to Herod's braggadocio, there are John's disciples who come after his death and personally carry his body to the tomb. It's an act usually relegated to the women, but these men are comfortable caring. These obscure characters in Mark 6 live lives characterized by sacrifice and principle and humility and caring. In the process, we see that it is their testimonies and not their testosterone levels that drive their lives.

Most of us probably would have not known the difference between Herod the Great, Herod Agrippa, and Herod Antipas before we walked into this sanctuary. I had forgotten. I had to consult several reference books to get them all straight. But you know what? Most of us don't care, do we? If I told you they were all famous and powerful rulers, would that peak your interest? No! We don't care, do we? On the other hand, we all know John the Baptist. We all know this is the one who spent his life pointing toward Jesus. This is the one who said, I have to decrease so that Jesus can increase. He lived a life driven not by testosterone but by his testimony and his faith.

I have heard that the word "ego" is actually an acronym for e—edging, g—God, o—out. Ego. Edging God out. That is what we do when driven by testosterone rather than by testimony. That is the result of being self-indulged with our own desires and our own opinions rather than humbly sacrificing ourselves to Christ.

My good friend, Cooter, called me two weeks ago. (There's a name that's filled with testosterone.) He said he was calling to check up on me, to see how I was doing. The conversation quickly moved, however, from my concerns and circumstances to his. Cooter was turning fifty this year.

"Jim," he said, "I own my own business (testosterone), I have cars and trucks in the garage (testosterone), a BMW motorcycle (testosterone), a beautiful wife (testosterone), and three great kids (testosterone). I've played baseball, coached baseball, and lived out most of my dreams (testosterone, testosterone, testosterone). I was sitting in church a couple of weeks ago, listening to the preacher and thinking to myself—I have all this stuff and I have done all this stuff, but what have I really said or given or done that matters or that has made a difference in this world?"

For the next fifteen minutes we talked about testimony. He had made an enormous difference in my life and the lives of many other people. He had not lived for himself alone. He had lived for family and friends and students and church and God. That's the difference. Manly men don't live driven by testosterone; they live driven by testimony.

I know what some of you are thinking. "Jim, I know it is Men's Day, but what about the ladies?"

Don't even get me started on their hormones—I'm not going there! What I *am* going to suggest is that we all give our lives to Christ. That we all live our lives for Christ. And may we all, above anything else, be driven by our testimonies.

GROWING UP WITH SOLOMON'S SONG

St. Valentine's Day
Song of Solomon 7:1–9

The Song of Solomon was a source of laughter during my childhood. I admit it. I was like most nine-, ten-, eleven-year-old prepubescent young boys. Anything anatomical was comical. And to mention a body part in a church service only heightened the hilarity.

So I received a spanking almost every holiday. On Palm Sunday, our pastor always read the Triumphal Entry story from the King James Version of the Bible, which does not use the word "donkey" as the mode of Jesus' transportation. As soon as the three-letter equine synonym left his lips, my brothers and I would all cover our mouths and try hard not to spew forth laughter. It always spewed. We got a spanking.

During the Christmas season, I dreaded the moment when our minister of music would ask us to sing the hymn numbered 118 in our hymnal—"What Child Is This." I knew we would soon arrive at the second verse, and again we would have to cover our mouths, try hard not to giggle, and end up sputtering into laughter. But as soon as the "ox and [three-letter-equine-synonym] before him bowed," we burst into laughter and earned yet another spanking. We were typical boys.

If I really wanted to tempt personal pain or wanted to get my little brother in trouble, then I would wait until the minister was halfway through his sermon, open my Bible to Song of Solomon, chapter 7, lay it in my brother's lap, and quickly point to verse 3. As soon as his eyes fell upon the female anatomical references couched in biblical text, he was covering his mouth and trying hard to hold in the laughter. Another spanking...for both of us. As a child, the Song of Solomon was a source of laughter for me.

As a teenager, the Song of Solomon became a source of dreams. Just read the words of this woman and how she speaks of her man. Listen to how she describes him. In chapter 2, she describes him as a young lover bounding over the hills, leaping over the mountains like a young stag. In chapter 5, she says his arms are rounded with gold-set jewels, his body is an ivory work encrusted with sapphires, his legs are alabaster columns set in bases of gold, and his voice is most sweet. These words became the source of my dreams.

I used to dream of finding a woman who would envision me like that. When I walked up, she would see me as the perfect physical specimen having the mind of an Einstein and the body of a god. (They say love is blind. I needed someone with severe sight problems and a vivid imagination.) I finally found her. Someone who worshiped the very ground I walked on. But then we graduated from high school and never saw each other again. You didn't think I was talking about my wife, did you? Oh, no. The moment I said, "mind of an Einstein and the body of a god," she was covering her mouth trying hard to hold in the laughter.

As a teenager, the Song of Solomon was a source of dreams. *In graduate school, the Song of Solomon became a source of study.* Synagogue and church have never been quite sure what to do with these seductive stanzas. But they are part of holy scripture, and the minister, every once in a while, has to read them in the process of worship or personal faith development.

Many Jewish people, throughout history, have chosen to read these texts as a symbolic expression of love between God and Israel. That almost makes it manageable. Centuries later, the church fathers baptized it and saw it as the symbolic expression of love between Christ and the church. This made it somewhat manageable for

Christians. There were saints in the life of the church—like Julia of Norwich and St. Francis—who felt these words were an expression of our own individual love and passion for the indwelling spirit of God. Again, a certain level of comfort was achieved through each of these perspectives, but this was still hard stuff to read during the Sunday morning worship hour! In our worship planning meeting this past Tuesday, the staff ministers were volunteering for worship leadership assignments. Everyone jumped at the gospel lesson, psalm, epistle lesson, and prayers. No one wanted to read the Old Testament lesson!

So, in our scholarly studies, we took the Song of Solomon and nestled it between the Writings and the Prophets—right after Ecclesiastes and right before Isaiah. It sits in a convenient little ecclesiastical crack where it can be ignored…most of the time.

For me, the Song of Solomon has been a source of laughter, dreams, and scholastic inquiry. *I have finally come to see the book as a source of permission—permission for passion.*

I cried at the end of the movie *A Beautiful Mind*. I cry every time I watch *The Sound of Music*. I laugh until my side hurts when I watch Bill Murray in *Caddy Shack*. In the fall, my car slows down a bit when I drive up Twin Pines Road and Briarcliff Road toward our church. As I cruise beneath the canopy of autumn leaves, I imagine them to be the beautifully painted ceiling of nature's finest cathedral. When I drive onto the church grounds, I exit my car and walk to our outdoor amphitheatre. I stop each morning and look at the azaleas and pines and crape myrtles. I just stand in wonder.

I think the reason I cry and laugh and look at these things so intently is because I don't want to lose my passion for the beautiful moments of life. Researchers tell us that the moment we see our lover walk into a room, both our heart rate and our blood pressure increase. I never want my heart rate to stay the same when my wife walks into a room.

The Song of Solomon gives me permission to be passionate about the beauty I see in life—the beauty I see in the people I love. Listen to the words again: "How graceful are your feet in sandals, O queenly maid. Your rounded thighs are like jewels, the work of a master hand. Your navel like a rounded bowl that never lacks mixed wine. Your belly a heap of wheat, circled with lilies...your breasts are like fawns...your neck like an ivory tower...your eyes like pools...how fair and how pleasant you are." What is it like to be looked at and loved like that? Realistically, this woman is not flawless as her lover claims. In chapter 1, she despises her own sun-darkened skin. In chapter 8, her brothers tease her concerning the same parts that her lover compliments over and over again.

Allow me to paraphrase the sentiment of Solomon as he speaks to the woman he loves. "I don't know what you see when you look in the mirror. And I'm not sure what other people see when they look at you. But when I look at you, this is what I see. How beautiful you are, my beloved."

Love is blind. No, I take that back. Love is not blind; it's just a passionate way of looking at things. In Genesis 2:18, God makes an incredible and perhaps confessional observation with regard to his human creation. He looks at the man and realizes the man is lonely. Even with the primordial presence of God, the man is lonely. God essentially confesses that God cannot meet all of humanity's needs. God created us to be social, emotional, and physical creatures. We crave and desire. We want to touch and be touched. We make our living as lawyers, doctors, teachers, bankers, and builders, but laughing and crying and loving and being loved...that's what we live for. Those are the passions of life.

The Song of Solomon gives us permission to pursue our passions and enjoy them—even see them as holy. Rather than denounce or deny the beauty in your lover or the beauty in God's world, see him or her as a gift. Bone of your bone, flesh of your flesh, world of your world, intended to bring joy.

At the end of every worship service, I invite you to unite your life with Christ and this church. When I extend that invitation, I am not calling you to profess faith in a God who wishes to diminish the passions of your life. But rather, I am calling you to a relationship with the God who wants you to enjoy passionately the moments and gifts you've been given. When I ask you to unite with this church, I am not calling you to a church that will discourage you from pursuing the passions of your life. But rather, I hope the church will encourage you to be passionate about your life and the things and people you love.

LENT AND EASTER

MY LIMITED MIND

1st Sunday of Lent
1 Peter 3:18–22

I am going to try to let my imagination run wild this morning. This is hard for me because I have a fairly narrow mind. When I read in 1 Peter 3:18 that Christ suffered, in my narrow mind I just see suffering. Again, I confess, this is due to the limits of my mind…the limit of my human imagination. *I just see suffering.*

Palm Sunday is weeks away. As we have in years past, we will spend part of our worship hour reading the complete crucifixion narrative—more than fifty-five verses of torturous text that never seems to end. After last year's service, one of our fellow parishioners exited the narthex and said to me, "I didn't like that reading."

"Why?" I asked. "Was it too long?"

"No," she responded. "It was too painful."

I confess: I'm like you. When I see the cross and when I read those fifty-five verses, I just see suffering. My mind focuses on nails and whips and spears and spit and laughing and slapping and mocking and thirst. I see suffering.

A medical doctor in Baxley, Georgia, is locally renowned for making classes and congregations cringe and cry as he presents the physical pain that was associated with death by crucifixion. Several times during my tenure at First Baptist Church in Baxley, people would ask me to invite him to come and share his presentation. I never did. Partly because it was hard enough for me to read the story as printed. I'm not sure I could manage the graphic details. I confess that, in my limited mind, I just see suffering.

Peter, however, has a much broader mind and a much more active imagination than me. *When Peter looks at the cross, he sees beneficial suffering.* This beneficial suffering is of particular interest to those who have been baptized. In fact, this may be the primary point of Peter's letter. In the first century, there were Christians who were suffering for their faith. In order to encourage them in the faith, Peter shows them there are positive results to negative suffering. He says to the first-century Christians, your suffering and your persecution will reap positive results. He uses language and phrases that we are very familiar with—they have become a part of the verbiage of the church. So if we were to read verse 18 again, we hear the expression of these familiar ideas: Jesus died for our sins, Jesus' atoning death, the righteous dying for the unrighteous, and the vicarious suffering that reconciles us to God. As a result, in our creeds, our statements of faith, our lectures, and our sermons, this language becomes the language of the church. It's what we say we believe.

But again, I must confess, my mind is limited. It is hard for me to imagine that one man's death can do all of that for me and for you. I have been raised in a church like most of you. For all of my life, I have heard it and I have said it and I have sung it—Jesus paid it all. All to him I owe. Sin had left a crimson stain. He washed it white as snow. What can wash away my sins? Nothing but the blood of Jesus. There is a fountain filled with blood drawn from Emmanuel's veins. And sinners who are plunged beneath that flood lose all their guilty stains.

The vicarious, atoning, reconciling work of God in Christ is an incredible image. My mind doesn't understand it, but I've accepted it. I have accepted that all who come to the cross, all who choose Christ, all who are part of the baptized will benefit gracefully from Christ's suffering.

But Peter is not through. Peter has a broad mind...a vivid imagination. His mind goes beyond this. He goes places I could never imagine going. Peter certainly asserts that Christ's suffering benefits the baptized. *But Peter goes on to say that Christ's suffering gracefully benefits the unbaptized.* God's love, Christ's death, the gospel is so powerful and so boundless and so complete that even the disobedient find redemption.

It's a strange story Peter tells. Jesus is put to death in verse 18. Nothing new so far. But, according to Peter, he was made alive in the spirit. Jesus then went and preached to the spirits in prison, who in former times did not obey God. These were the spirits of those destroyed in the flood. These were the spirits of those whose sins were so grievous they prompted God to regret the creation of humankind. Noah and his family were saved. They moved through the waters. They prefigured baptism. The spirits in prison were the damned.

This short passage is often referred to as the harrowing of hell. It is mentioned in the Apostle's Creed. It is part of the lectionary text for today. It will probably be ignored in most Christian churches, however. The average preacher will address the gospel lesson instead, or the Old Testament lesson, or any other lesson! And there is a part of me that understands their avoidance and hesitation.

Most theologians want to avoid this verse. While on the one hand some theologians will vehemently espouse that every word of scripture must be taken seriously, when they come to 1 Peter 3, well, as one of my dear friends told me last week, "Since it's rarely mentioned scripture, it should not bear significantly on any of our doctrines." I thought that was strange. Since it's rarely mentioned, it doesn't really matter?

Can I ask you a question? Just a matter of personal curiosity. If one of your family members—child, husband, wife, parent, grandparent—turned into a werewolf just one night out of the year, would you downplay its significance since it only happens once a year? No! Wouldn't it be just the opposite? Wouldn't you say this is the very center of who he or she is? This is the one characteristic that differentiates that special person from the rest of the human population. You would want to find out what it means!

Here's what Peter says it means. The power of Christ, the power of the gospel, the power of God's love knows no boundaries and no limits. Yes, those who move through the water—like Noah and you and me and all the other baptized believers—we know and benefit from God's grace. But Peter holds up this second image—those who have not moved through the water, those who are disobedient during God's long-suffering patience, are also beneficiaries of God's grace. I'll be honest with you. Peter's argument and Peter's mind and Peter's imagination are much broader than mine. My mind is much too limited to grasp such grace.

In Matthew's gospel, we find a strange story. Jesus takes his last breath on the cross and dies. Immediately, the earth begins to rumble. Graves are opened and the righteous come forth and testify. Do you remember that story? Peter says, oh no, it goes further and deeper than that. It's not just the righteous whose graves are opened; Christ descends and bursts hell wide open, and even the unbaptized are redeemed. The power of the gospel—the power of God's grace—pursued the most disobedient of folks and brought them to redemption. Those decadent human souls who suffered the ravages of the flood…Christ pursues them into the very cracks and crevices of Sheol and brings them to redemption.

How did the psalmist say it? "If I soar to the heights, you are there. If I make my bed in Hell, you are there." That's a little beyond my imagination.

There have been others whose imaginations were almost as wild as Peter's. Clarence Jordan imagined it. Have you ever heard Clarence Jordan's sermon on the ten coins? Remember the lady who had ten coins and she lost one of them? Clarence Jordan had a wonderful sermon where he prompted the listener to think. "How long," he asked, "did she look for that coin? Did she look for it until her lamp burnt out? No. Did she look for it until her broom wore out? No. Did she look for it until her husband came home and asked why supper wasn't on the table? No. The scripture says she looked for it until she found it."

How did the Apostle Paul say it? "We have not yet begun to imagine the height and the depth and the breath of God's love." Paul knew the limits of our imagination. He knew that it would be a huge human stretch to embrace the expanse of God's persistent, patient, graceful love. It's beyond my imagination.

After *Background Music*, the book I wrote for my oldest daughter when she graduated from high school, was published, a parishioner asked me a poignant question. "Jim," she said, "I have read your book. I enjoyed almost all of it. But I was left with one nagging question. Are you a Universalist?"

I laughingly responded, "Are you kidding? Are you kidding? Me, a Universalist? Are you kidding? My mother was a Jew. Now we Jews know that we are God's chosen people and we are just hoping you Gentiles get in. My mother married a Roman Catholic. I was christened into the Roman Catholic Church. We Roman Catholics know that we are the one true church and we are just hoping you Protestants get in. I was adopted by a Southern Baptist family in southern Arkansas. We know that only Southern Baptists go to heaven; we just hope everybody else gets in. Me, a Universalist? Are you kidding? I've spent my whole life learning about "them" and "us." Who's "in" and who's "out." I can't imagine being a Universalist. However, I believe God might be one."

Clarence Jordan imagined it. The writer of the book of Hebrews imagined it when he proposed that Christ went into the sanctuary and offered a perfect sacrifice *once for all*. John, in his first letter, imagined it when he said that Christ is the expiation for our sins, and not for our sins only, *but for the sins of the whole cosmos—the whole world*. Peter imagined it when he said it wasn't just the obedient but the disobedient, not just the baptized but the unbaptized, not just the select, but all gracefully benefit from Christ's suffering. That is beyond my imagination.

This is what I know. I know that God absolutely loves us. I know that God is absolutely committed to our redemption. I know that God has absolutely proven his love toward us and demonstrated it by giving his Son, Jesus Christ. I know that the quicker we embrace that love, the quicker we will begin living lives that are filled with joy and purpose. Every day that we live without acknowledging that love—every day—has a little bit of hell in it.

BREAD ENOUGH

2nd Sunday of Lent
Mark 8:1–21

Why do we find it so hard to trust God? Through the twists and the turns and the problems and the pains of our lives, why do we find it so hard to trust God?

I spent New Year's Eve at the home of some friends. There was another minister there who does a wonderful impersonation of Billy Graham. I am not going to try to mimic his impersonation this morning, but he did tell a story in the process of his impersonation that I'm sure most of us have heard Billy Graham or someone repeating at one time or another. It was about a man who wandered much too close to a cliff, fell over the edge of the cliff, and while plummeting to his certain death, reached out and just happened to catch onto a frail, fragile branch sticking out of the mountain wall. He hung there for a while and then he started screaming for help. He finally heard a voice from above say, "Let go of the branch."

"Who said that?" the man fearfully but hopefully asked.

"This is God, your Father, in heaven. I'm telling you that all will be well. Let go of the branch."

The man thought for a moment, then screamed back, "Is there anybody else up there?"

Why do we find it so hard to trust God? *The most obvious reason presented in today's text is that we simply forget God's powerful past.* This is a point that Jesus pushes in the story today. The disciples are worried because they have forgotten to bring bread enough for a few disciples and their master Jesus. Jesus essentially says to them, when he realizes what they are worried about, "Are you kidding? Are you kidding?" At the end of verse 18, he says, "Do you not remember that back in chapter 6, I took just a few loaves and a few fishes and fed 5,000 people and we had 12 baskets left over? And just a few verses ago, before we hit the lake, I fed 4,000 people with about the same menu and we had 7 baskets full left over? Are you kidding? Just in the few chapters that we have been together—in the little bit of time that we have been together—I've raised a child from the dead, walked on water, healed a paralytic, healed a leper, and healed a demoniac. Are you kidding? Are you really worried about your daily bread?"

God's people in every generation have had to be reminded of God's powerful past. Every time the Israelites hit a rough spot, they had to be reminded of that great exodus experience and all of God's powerful displays of power that occurred in that chapter of their lives. The disciples were no different and we are no different. We struggle to trust God because we too quickly forget God's powerful past.

A little boy wanted to go to his friend's birthday party that was about half a mile down the street. His dad had promised him that he could walk to the party, but when the day of the party came, there was a snowstorm of almost blizzard conditions. His dad told him, "There is no way that we can drive there and there is no way that I'm going to let you walk to that party this morning."

The little boy begged and begged and begged. "But all of my other friends are going to be there, and I don't want to miss it. Dad, please let me go. Please let me go!"

Finally, much to the surprise of the little boy (and much to the surprise of his mother), the dad said, "Okay, you can go."

The little boy bundled up and opened the front door. A bitter wind hit him in the face. He made his way to the sidewalk. He took a right turn and leaned into the wind, walking as strongly and firmly as he could through the snow. The snow was blowing so hard that he could just barely see in front of him, but in twice the time it should have taken him, he finally made it to his little friend's front door. As he walked up to the porch and rang the doorbell, he turned around just to glance at the storm one more time. When he turned, he saw the silhouette of his father walking back down the sidewalk. His dad had followed him all the way there. He had been with him all the way. It is important for us to glance back every once in a while and see the shadowy silhouette of our Father who walks with us.

When I'm visiting the hospitals or funeral homes or just in homes where there has been a crisis, I have one phrase that almost always makes it into my prayers. Many of you have heard it. It is, "God, we know that you have walked with us through every chapter of the past, and we know that you will walk with us through this one." It's part of what we affirm when we celebrate communion. A broken body, poured out blood—every time you eat it, every time you drink it, glance backwards and remember to trust God because of God's powerful past.

There is a greater source of mistrust that is more subtly addressed in this text. *It's not just that we forget about God's powerful past, but many of us don't trust God because we can't accept God's grace in the present.* It is hard for us to believe that God's grace is readily available for our lives.

I had an appointment recently with a member of our community. He was going through a tough time. In the course of that conversation I told him that our associate pastor has a verse that hangs on the wall in his office. It's Jeremiah 29:11. I told him, "This week before we get together again, I want you to go home and read that verse. I would like for you to write it down on an index card and lay it on your desk at your office and read it every day."

"What does it say?" he asked.

"It says, 'I know the plans I have for you, said the Lord. Plans for good and not for harm. A future where there is hope.'"

He looked deep into my eyes and said, "I don't believe that. I believe God is out to get me."

Jesus and his disciples had come to a wonderful, intimate, private moment. Jesus was thinking, *5,000 were fed with bread. 4,000 were fed with bread.* And, in a moment of insight, prompted by these prior events, Jesus shared a heavenly truth with his disciples. "Listen," he said, "I want you to avoid the yeast of the Pharisees. Their hypocrisy can easily creep into your life. I also want you to avoid the yeast of Herod. His worldliness can easily creep into your life. These things are like yeast in bread. It's a little thing, but it has a profound impact."

As soon as these words came out of his mouth, the disciples looked at each other and said, "He's mad because we didn't bring any bread, isn't he?" They missed a heavenly moment because they were worried about a mistake they had made—a mistake that wasn't anywhere on Jesus' radar.

We can't accept God's grace in the present. We find it hard to believe that the God of heaven absolutely accepts us and absolutely loves us. Our mistakes are nowhere on God's radar. They have been cast as far as the east is from the west. They have been thrown into the sea of forgetfulness. They have been covered by the blood of Christ—they are remembered no more. We think that God is out to get us, and the truth is that God is just out to love us. That is the good news of the gospel.

I'm afraid that we have abusively dangled humanity over the horrors of hell for so long and preached to provoke guilt in people for so long that it is hard to accept the great gift of grace.

It's a classic situation seen in many movies and commercials. A beautiful girl is on one side of the room, her every move exuding elegance. On the other side of the room, there is a man who looks like he has struggled to get a date his whole life. He is awkward, uncomfortable, and looks completely out of place. But this beautiful woman looks his way and winks and smiles. What does he do? He looks over his shoulder, looks around, thinks she must be winking at somebody else. And then he silently mouths a monosyllabic question. "Me?" She says, "Yes, you."

God is winking at us. God was winking at those breadless disciples who were seated in the boat. The same disciples who would later be seated around the table: one who would deny him, one who would betray him, the rest who would desert him. He was winking at all of them and saying, "Trust me. You wouldn't be here if I didn't love you. Trust me."

How did the poet say it?

Trust Him when dark doubts assail thee
Trust Him when thy strength is small,
Trust Him when to simply trust Him
Seems the hardest thing of all

Trust Him, He is ever faithful;
Trust Him for His will is best;
Trust Him, for the heart of Jesus
Is the only place of rest. (anonymous)

Trust the God who has a powerful past. Trust the God who has a great grace for your present. Trust God and know there will always be bread enough.

WHEN WE TALK ABOUT US...
LET'S BE HONEST

3rd Sunday of Lent
John 4:27–42

Night questions. Nicodemus came to Jesus by night to ask his questions. That is what the Gospel of John tells us in chapter 3. And being a person of high religious standing, it wouldn't have been appropriate for Nicodemus to do otherwise. Number one—to even admit that he had any questions. Number two—certainly to ask Jesus for the answers. And so, being who he was at the time he lived, Nicodemus came to Jesus by night for a little intellectual, theological one-on-one. That's John 3. That's night questions.

Today's text, John 4, is at the other end of the spectrum. A Samaritan woman meets Jesus in the middle of the heat of the day. I'm sure you have heard the interpretations and the assumptions. Typically in that culture, women gathered together as a group and walked to the well in the cool of the morning to draw their water. It was a practical time for the family as well as a social time for these women. But, if you have had five husbands and you are presently not married to the person you are living with—well, you go to the well in the middle of the heat of the day...in the heat of the day...alone.

Life had hit this lady square in the face. It sounds like she had truly tried. In fact, over and over and over and over again she had tried. It just seems like her dreams and her prayers and her greatest hopes were never realized.

When you are that beat up or when you are that beat down, you have little pride and little pretense left. So if you've got questions, you just ask them in the middle of the day, out loud. It doesn't matter anyway. Most of the questions this lady asked at the well seemed kind of simple, maybe even trite. But the truth is that they are fairly profound questions when you listen to them. I would imagine they are the kind of questions all of us ask at some point in our lifetime. Questions like the one she asks in verse 9, when she says, *"Is God really gracious enough to love me?"*

I know that is not exactly the way she said it, but that is the essence of her inquiry. She looks at Jesus, who has asked her for a cup of water, and she says, "How is it that you, a Jew, ask me, a Samaritan woman, for a drink of water? Jews have nothing to do with us." At the heart of that question was the thought, "Is God really gracious enough to love me?"

Tony Campolo, the always energetic professor, preacher, and author, tells a story of walking down the sidewalk in a large city after attending a speaking engagement. He was approached by a lady of the evening. She came to him and asked, "How would you like a date?"

He said, out of sheer curiosity, "How much does a date cost?"

"$20," she offered.

"Are you kidding? That's not enough!" Campolo responded with shock.

"Okay, $30."

"You are not even close."

"$50?"

"More," he said.

"$100!"

He looked at her and said, "Lady, you have no idea how much you are worth to God." He went on to tell her that she was selling herself way too cheap, and that God had paid a much higher price for her through his Son, Jesus Christ.

One of the greatest temptations we face as humans is the temptation of self-rejection. After all, that is what all the voices scream at us. Voices outside of us tell us we are failures, or we are worthless, or we are no good unless we prove otherwise by winning or succeeding or making it to the top. And if the voices outside of us are not loud enough, then there are voices inside of us constantly reminding us of our past shortcomings and potential failures.

Here is the good news of the gospel: God knows you and God is gracious enough to love you. It is no accident that the first words Jesus heard after his baptism were "This is my beloved Son in whom I am well pleased." God knew about all the other voices Jesus would have to listen to. It is not by accident that every time we baptize a person in this chapel, the first words I say to them when they come out of the water are "You are God's beloved child in whom God is well pleased." I know the voices from the outside and the inside that every one of those believers is going to have to hear.

The answer to the Samaritan woman's inquiry is yes, God is gracious enough to love you. It is the same answer that was heard by the prodigal son when he looked around and saw himself seated in a pigsty and wondered if his dad could ever love him again. Yes, God is gracious enough to love you. The same answer the adulteress woman heard when caught in the very act and thrown in the middle of a self-righteous crowd. I'm sure she was thinking, "Could God ever love me?" Yes, God is gracious enough to love you.

The thief who looked over at another thief and said, "Why in the world are you ridiculing this man? He's done nothing. We deserve what we are getting." And the answer was still yes, God is gracious enough to love you. For the Samaritan woman who had five failed marriages and was sitting alone in the middle of the heat of the day, asking that same question—the answer was yes.

Of course, there was a second question, and it seems almost as trite. "You don't even have a cup or a bucket. How in the world are you going to get any water? Are you greater than our ancestor Jacob, who dug this well?" The first question addresses the goodness and the graciousness of God. The second question addresses God's power. *Is God powerful enough to change my life?*

Are you greater than our ancestor Jacob who dug this well and fed all of our flocks for all of these years? It's not literally what she is asking, but it is certainly the question in her heart. How powerful are you? Jesus must have smiled when he responded, "If you only knew who you were talking to. You would have asked for some water and I would have given you water that would have changed your life forever. Do you know who you are talking to?"

I know God is gracious enough to love me, but is he powerful enough to change me and help me? That's a completely different question.

It's the season of Lent. During these first days of Lent, it has not been difficult for me to look inside myself and search myself and discover some of my needs. It hasn't even been that difficult for me to look at Christ on the cross and recognize God's gracious love and acceptance of me. But whether or not I'm going to have the power to change after these forty days—that's the hard part, isn't it? Is God powerful enough to change me?

In our seminary apartment building, Bimbo was our downstairs neighbor. That wasn't his real name. His real name was Douglas, but everyone called him Bimbo. He was not much of a theologian or a student, but he was a master of all things mechanical.

When we moved into the apartment above him, we unpacked all our boxes and put all the appliances in their appropriate places on the counter. We turned on everything that was supposed to be turned on, but as time went by, we realized that the clothes dryer was not working. Of course, being the mechanical genius that I am, I pushed every knob on the dryer and turned every dial. I opened the door and slammed the door and opened the door and slammed the door. I even reached in and grabbed that big barrel thing and gave it a good spin, thinking it was like one of those old airplanes that needed a spin of the propeller to get started. Nothing worked, so we called Bimbo. Bimbo came upstairs. He pushed the buttons and turned the knobs and he opened the door and closed the door. Then he pulled the dryer away from the wall, reached down, picked up the cord, and plugged it into the outlet. He pushed the button and it turned on. He turned around and said to me with the straightest face he could muster, "Now, as long as you keep it plugged in, it will work just fine." Maybe he was a better theologian than we knew.

Is God powerful enough to change me? As long as you keep it plugged in, it works just fine. I have a friend named John. We live in separate cities now, and he has been sober for several years. He has told me before, "I'm not sober because fifteen years ago I decided to be sober." He said, "I'm sober because every morning I get up and I ask my higher power to help me." It works just fine if you keep it plugged in.

Every morning I have to get up and ask my higher power to help me with my children, help me with my attitude, help me with my work, and help me with my struggles. I have found that as long as I make it a daily prayer, and as long as Sunday after Sunday I'm in this place, and Wednesday after Wednesday I gather for prayer—as long as I keep it plugged in, God's power is there to help me and change me.

Maybe that is what forty days of Lent and daytime questions are all about. Is God gracious enough to love me? Absolutely. Is God powerful enough to change me? Absolutely. We simply have to be willing to receive the love and power.

MY GREATEST NEED

4th Sunday of Lent
Ephesians 2:1–10

We have read three interesting but seemingly unrelated biblical texts on this fourth Sunday of Lent. We have read from Ephesians 2, which sounds and feels natural. After all, this is Lent, and part of the Lenten experience is our desperate need for God's mercy. Our gospel lesson, however, was from Luke 1—a story we tend to associate with the Christmas season—the angelic annunciation of Christ's birth to the virgin Mary. Why read Luke 1? Today is more than just the fourth Sunday of Lent; this is also Annunciation Sunday. The Sunday that is the closest to March 25, which is nine months before December 25, and now you're catching on.

The fourth Sunday of Lent is also celebrated as Laughter Sunday in some Christian traditions. After Lent had been established as part of the church's seasonal calendar, church leaders observed that it was terribly depressing to some people. (Go figure.) Forty days of soul searching and repentance, realizing that you are not everything you wish you were and not everything God wished you were—people began to get depressed. These perceptive church leaders decided that what we needed was a psychological break—day of relaxation and refreshment and laughter—in the middle of this otherwise morose period of penance. And so they designated the fourth Sunday of Lent Laughter Sunday. It is in the spirit of Laughter Sunday that we read the Old Testament lesson from the book of Ecclesiastes: "...eat, drink, and be merry." In fact, this may be one of my greatest needs—laughter.

I need to laugh more. I think we all need to laugh more, especially we adults. Children laugh an average 150 times a day. Adults? Less than 15 times a day. I think the writer of Ecclesiastes was on to something. (A bit depressing, like the Lenten season, but on to something.) Life is so short. We all are going to end up in a grave anyway. We might as well enjoy every measure and every moment of time and health and wealth that we are given. Eat, drink, and laugh!

The writer of Ecclesiastes is not the only person to say this. The book of Proverbs states on numerous occasions that a laughing heart is a continual feast and that merriment is good for the heart. Even the editors of *Reader's Digest* know that laughter is the best medicine. We all need to laugh more. I need to laugh more.

Knowing that Laughter Sunday was on the way, I was delighted with the jokes and anecdotes you have sent me, via e-mail, in recent days. They were all funny. I can't share any of them with the congregation, but they were all funny!

Once, I shared an inappropriate joke during a former pastorate. I was in attendance at the weekly Saturday night Rook game. The conversation had declined into decadence, the way card conversations often do, and in the fervor and frenzy of the moment, I decided to tell "the joke." As soon as I said the punch line, everyone stared at me wide-eyed, jaws dropped for about two seconds and then...they burst into laughter. I'm not sure if the joke was that funny or it was just the fact that the preacher was the one who told the joke. But they laughed until they couldn't breathe! The next morning was Sunday. Parishioners filed into their familiar pews. Two deacons, however, were seated in the balcony. No one ever sat in the balcony. We sang our hymns, welcomed our visitors, prayed our prayers, shared our announcements, collected our offerings, and listened to the choir's anthem. The time had come for me to preach. As I approached the pulpit, the two deacons who were seated in the balcony stood up and unrolled a large, white piece of butcher paper that read *Tell the joke, Jim!* This time, *I* was silent for two seconds with wide eyes and a dropped jaw. The congregation, hearing the rattle of paper and seeing the focal direction of my eyes, turned and looked and read. Everyone burst into laughter except the children, who didn't have a clue what was going on. It became one of those memorable moments in the unwritten history of Mount Olivet Baptist Church.

We were able to laugh at that joke, and laugh at and with one another, because there existed a deep sense of trust and love between us. Maybe that is really the issue. Maybe that is really the need. Children laugh more than adults do. Is it because they are still at a place in life where ignorance is bliss and their naiveté can conjure complete trust? Is it because they know that no matter what they say or do they are still going to be loved?

I think I need to laugh more. More than that, however, *I need to trust more.* We laugh and eat and drink with people we trust. Trust prompts heartfelt laughter. This great need brings us to Luke 1—the annunciation text. I used to read this story, and like most of you, I imagined a splendid angel appearing in the middle of a clear starlit evening and talking to poor, pure, humble Mary—maybe even hearing the Beatles playing "Let It Be" in the background (that part probably occurs only in my imagination, not yours). But have I truly described the ambiance of that moment? Or was Mary's obedience mixed with a little more terror and ambivalence? After all, "Fear not" is a necessary part of the angelic greeting.

This past Thursday night, I attended a presentation of *The Vagina Monologues.* My oldest daughter had a role in this poignant, often considered controversial play, and she had invited me to attend. I did. This series of monologues is intended to communicate the struggles, challenges, misunderstandings, stereotypes, and abuses that women have endured and continue to endure in our world. I learned a lot Thursday night—things that somewhere, in the back of my statistical mind, I thought I knew.

During the course of this theatric presentation and the conversation that followed, I learned that one in six women in the

United States has either been the victim of rape or an attempted rape. Fifty percent of those women are under the age of eighteen. Fifteen hundred women a year are killed, in our nation, by their boyfriends or their husbands. Four million cases of domestic abuse are reported every year, and it's estimated that only 90 percent of incidents of abuse are ever reported. All of this is happening in twenty-first-century America!

I went home Thursday night and read Luke 1 again; I heard it differently. The angel came to Mary and said, "The spirit of God *will* hover over you. You *will* conceive and you *will* bear a child and you *will* call him Jesus." Can you imagine what that sounded like in a less civilized, first-century culture where gods and men did whatever they wanted to and with women? And how old was Mary? Fourteen? Fifteen? Sixteen? Seventeen? I have always pictured her as just a pure, obedient little child. But after Thursday night, I realize this was a trusting young woman—someone who trusted the words that were spoken to her—even when every fiber of her being probably argued against it...should have argued against it. She trusted. And within that same chapter, trust allowed her to burst into song and laughter. Fear produces tears. Trust prompts laughter.

The running track at the Wellness Center is elevated over the gymnasium's swimming pool. One Sunday afternoon, months ago, I was running on the track while the children's swim class was in progress below. As I made a lap around the track, I saw a little child clinging to his mother's shoulder, screaming, "It's too deep! It's too deep!" Everyone on the track slowed and watched the ensuing drama. The mother finally calmed the child and was able to say confidently and caringly, "Honey, there is no spot in this pool where I can't touch the bottom. I'm going to stay with you. I promise." And she did.

That's my greatest need—to trust God more. To hear the words of Ephesians 2, when God says, "While you were dead in your trespasses, my mercy was so immeasurable that I lifted you up just so people could see how merciful I am. By grace you have been saved, Jim Dant. Nothing you have done can keep you away from it. Nothing you have ever done or will do will help you earn it. It is my absolute, free gift to you…to the world."

When I am at my worst and when life's circumstances are at their worst, I need to trust that there is no place in this world where God cannot touch bottom. God has promised to stay with us. Trust God more. And since we are all in this together, we might as well trust each other more…and feel free to laugh.

THE LAND OF BEGINNING AGAIN

5th Sunday of Lent
John 8:1–11

John 8:1–11 is a familiar story. We have all heard it before. Scholars have challenged whether or not this passage should be part of John's gospel or at least if it was in the earliest text of the gospel.

In some of your Bibles, this story is set apart in brackets. In some of your Bibles, there is a footnote indicating this story has been placed in an appendix. In other Bibles, the story is omitted with no explanation.

The scholarly concern is not without good reason. The earliest manuscripts we have of the Gospel of John do not include this story. There are words in this story that do not appear anywhere else in the Gospel of John. This story contains the only reference to the Mt. of Olives in the Gospel of John. This is the only mention of the scribes in the Gospel of John. Jesus is called a teacher in this story. While that title is often attributed to him in other gospels—you guessed it—this is the only time in the Gospel of John. The context of this story is awkward. Dispute, argument, and theological bantering with the scribes and Pharisees occur quite often in the other gospels, but this is the only occurrence of such in the Gospel of John. With all this evidence (and even more that we are not going to hash out this morning), scholars have challenged whether this story truly belongs in the Gospel of John. Of course, this is not the only challenge associated with this text.

When you read the story, you quickly notice that the Pharisees are challenging Jesus. I have already stated this is typical in the other gospels. In Matthew, Mark, and Luke, the religious leaders bring Jesus a coin and question him about the appropriate approach to government taxation. The writers make it clear that their question is intended to put him at odds with Rome. Another leader poses a question about marriage, multiple marriages, death, levitical law, the afterlife, and resurrection. (Really, it's complicated.) The purpose is clear, however. The religious leaders are seeking to set Jesus at odds with the Sadducees and Pharisees.

In today's story, a woman has been caught in the act of adultery. The religious leaders come to Jesus requesting his legal insight with regard to the situation. After all, they assert, the law says she should be stoned. Again, their interest was nothing more than a trap...a trick...a challenge. If Jesus said to stone her, he would be usurping Roman authority. If he chose mercy, he would be circumventing their misinformed application of Jewish law. (The law states that a "man" caught in adultery was to be stoned. No mention is made of the woman. But that's another sermon for another day.) I think they finally thought to themselves, *We've got him this time.*

But it never works. We can't challenge God. It's like challenging Ken Jennings on *Jeopardy*—you can't beat him; you might as well go home. It's like challenging Marilyn vos Savant in *Parade Magazine*; you know she has all the right answers. It's like Cricket Spencer challenging Dusty Rhodes; he's not going to win. Do you know who Dusty Rhodes is? He is—was—a professional wrestling phenomenon. Do you know who Cricket Spencer is? Cricket attended fifth grade with me. He made me look like Charles Atlas and Arnold Schwarzenegger put together. We called him Cricket because, well, he looked like a cricket—little bitty legs and little bitty arms. Dusty Rhodes brought his wrestling show and wrestling ring to our school gymnasium during my fifth grade year. (And that was when wrestling was real.) We all went to see him. Between matches, he chose one kid in the audience to come into the ring and wrestle him. It was the scrappiest kid in the audience. Cricket climbed into the ring. The match was a joke, but Dusty was graceful. The scribes challenged Jesus. The match was a joke; Jesus was graceful.

When Jesus is posed this wonderful question, he just ignores them. He squats down, starts doodling in the dirt, hoping they will just go away. When he finally does stand up, he doesn't go for a knockout punch. He just nudges them. "Let the one without sin throw the first punch," he says. You can't challenge God.

The real point of this story seems to be that God can challenge us. Jesus challenged the Pharisees. After inviting the sinless to take a swing, he knelt down and started doodling in the dirt again. There is a huge difference between Jesus and humanity in this text. The Pharisees are using the law and the woman. The law is their weapon. The woman is just an object. Jesus on the other hand loves the law and the woman. Jesus refuses to use the law to inflict harm on humanity, and he refuses to use the woman as an interpretive guinea pig for the law. The law is sacred, meant for our health and betterment. The woman was human, a beloved child of God. Jesus knew that none of us could survive the law without grace. God's will is for us to survive. So God challenges the Pharisees to contemplate the need for grace in their own lives. Let the one who is without sin cast the first stone.

I was driving back from Brunswick, Georgia, to Macon, Georgia, on Highway 341 last weekend. As I was coming through Jesup, I was flipping through the frequencies on the lower end of the radio dial. Finally finding something other than static, I picked up a loud, voracious preacher. He was railing against those adulterers and homosexuals and fornicators who live in Atlanta. (Because we know that is where they all live. All the adulterers and homosexuals and fornicators are in Atlanta. There aren't any in Jesup, Georgia.) He went through this long, punitive paragraph and finally screamed, "I'm glad we are not like those sinners!"

I think this was Jesus' point when he said for the sinless to cast the first stone. I think this is what Jesus was saying. He was saying,

"You know, guys, you are more like her than you are different from her." None of us would survive the law without grace.

Of course, when they are all gone and only Jesus and the woman are left, there is one more challenge to be thrown down. *Jesus challenges the woman.* He stands up and asks her, "Where are your accusers?" She says, "There are none." Jesus says to her, (listen closely), "Neither do I condemn you. I do not condemn you. I do not condemn you." The only person in this story who could have thrown a rock...does not. Listen to the words. "You are not condemned."

The primary difference between the Pharisees and Jesus is that they wished to condemn, and he wished to forgive. They knew the thrill of condemning (and it can be thrilling). Jesus knew the thrill of forgiving. He wanted this woman to know the thrill of being forgiven, the thrill of having a second and a third and a hundredth chance.

His final words to her? Go and sin no more. This was not a threat. Jesus was not saying, "Now if you sin again, I'm taking all this forgiveness and grace and love back." No. This was Jesus' way of saying that she had another chance. Life begins anew today. You may feel that you have messed up everything, but life is not finished yet.

Louisa Fletcher Tarkington spoke for most of us...all of us:

> How I wish there was some wonderful place
> Called the Land of Beginning Again
> Where all of our mistakes and all of our heartaches
> And all of our selfish grief could be dropped
> Like a shabby old coat at the door and never put on again.

If you are looking for a place like that, you have come to the right place. The gospel does not say that broken laws and broken hearts and broken promises do not matter; they do. Pain and scars are real. The gospel does say, however, that every person has a future as well as a past. And Jesus is not as interested in where we have been as he is in where we could be.

So it is with good reason that scholars have challenged whether John 8:1–11 belongs in this gospel. But as for me, I'm glad it's there. My self-righteousness needs to be challenged every once in a while. And every once in a while, I need to hear about the land of beginning again.

THE GOSPEL ACCORDING TO STEPHEN HAWKING

Palm Sunday
April 4, 2004

The gospel according to Stephen Hawking. Stephen Hawking speaks with a computer-generated voice. He is bound to a wheelchair due to the toll that Lou Gehrig's Disease has taken on his body. Despite the limits of his physical frame, he constantly wears a coy smile, as if he knows something that we do not. And, in fact, he probably does. Mr. Hawking is a renowned physicist. From his wheelchair, he has generated some of the deepest scientific thought of our time. He, along with other physicists, has been amending—at times reversing—many of the ideas held for decades by the scientific community.

One of those ideas is the Law of Impenetrability. It's not as confusing as it sounds. This law essentially states that two objects cannot occupy the same space at the same time. That's pretty simple, right? But according to Mr. Hawking, many of his colleagues, some complex experiments with light particles, and the new theories of quantum physics, this law may be wrong. Two objects may, in fact, be able to occupy the same space at the same time. I would love to explain this to you, but I refuse to try. Not because of your ignorance, but because of mine.

I'm not sure I completely understand it. But I'm not going to allow Stephen Hawking's coy smile to make me feel bad or unintelligent. Why? Because his analytical assertions are not incredibly novel. The church has known for centuries that this law was wrong. We see evidence to the contrary every year—the Sunday before Easter. It is a day on the liturgical calendar that bears two names. It is Palm Sunday, and it is also Passion Sunday. Both realities occupy the same space at the same time. We wave palms of praise and at the same time we begin to feel pain of the passion.

Truth be known, we like the old law of physics better. We like to choose one or the other to occupy this space. We don't want them both in the same space at the same time. In fact, if we had a choice between palms and passion, you know what we would choose. We would choose palms.

We would choose palms. After all, everybody loves a celebration. Everybody loves a parade. Go to most churches on the Sunday before Easter, and they will be focusing on the palms, the parade, and the celebration.

The church has endeared herself to holiday festivities. At Christmas, we love shepherds dressed up in bathrobes and angels with glitter-covered cardboard wings. At Eastertide, we want our children waving palm branches down the center aisle of the church, hunting for Easter eggs on Saturday, and singing those great hymns of praise on Easter Sunday. We choose palms.

As a result, Palm Sunday, in many Christian traditions, has lost its sense of passion. Rather than a time of reverent—perhaps even painful—preparation and reflection, it has become the dress rehearsal before next week's resurrection celebration. It's like a scrimmage game before Easter Sunday. It's a time that has become exclusively devoted to joy and celebration and happiness and wonder. Yet, in the back of our minds, we know that passion is just around the corner. Crucifixion is just around the corner. But we tell ourselves that we know how the story ends. So why dwell on the dark parts? If we have a choice between palms and passion on this day, let's chose palms.

I think it is just part of our nature. Have you ever read the Victorian versions of Shakespeare's plays? During the Victorian era, the endings of Shakespeare's plays were drastically revised. The readers of that pristine era did not like the tragedies and their horrific, frustrating finales. So they rewrote them. *Hamlet* ends happily ever after. *Macbeth* ends happily ever after. At the end of *Romeo and Juliet*, the lovers survive their near-fatal wounds and potions. They rise from their deathbeds to marry and, yes, live happily ever after. Even their extended families—the rivaling Montagues and Capulets—become best of friends! Given the choice between palms and passion, we choose palms.

Maybe it's not just our nature. Maybe we just like shorter stories. Each year we begin our service by reading, in unison or responsively, the palm narrative. Jesus rides into Jerusalem on the back of a donkey, heralded by screaming fans, and the whole thing takes ten to twelve verses. Later in our service, we read the passion narrative in like manner. Well over fifty verses of trials, torture, pain, abandonment, and death. I've watched your faces each year. The reading of the passion is much more laborious than the reading of the palms.

Of course, maybe it's just the content. After all, it is much easier for us to exclaim, "Blessed is he who comes in the name of the Lord! Hallelujah!" than to scream, "Crucify him! Crucify him!" We choose palms.

Peter Gomes, the university chaplain at Harvard University, has sarcastically suggested that we go ahead and take the passion out of Palm Sunday. He concludes—again with tongue in cheek—that we should save all the suffering for those faithful, few, moral masochists who show up for Good Friday services. We choose palms.

Deep down, however, we know that the Law of Impenetrability is wrong. Two objects can occupy the same space at the same time. This day has to be a day for the celebration of palms *and* passion.

We must also choose passion. It's the only way the teachings of Jesus make sense. How did Jesus say it? In the world, you will have tribulation, but be of good cheer. I have overcome the world—palms and passion. Happy are those who are persecuted for my namesake—palms and passion. If you want to save your life, you must lose it—palms and passion.

It is the only way the life and death of Jesus make any sense. We must keep these two ideas close together. What do we call the Friday before Easter? Good Friday? What do we call Jesus? Righteous King, Suffering Servant, Lion of Judah, the Lamb that is slain, the crucified Christ—palms...passion.

It is really the only way our lives can make any sense. We must allow for and understand the coexistence of joy and pain in the Christian faith—palms and passion.

I hear it at the funeral home all the time. "I know she is in a better place, but I hurt." Palms and passion. I heard it in the hospital last week. While visiting a dear friend who is suffering from cancer and battling through the process of chemotherapy, I received a lesson in quantum physics...or at least quantum spirituality. With her frail hand in mine, my friend—weakly speaking in whispers—assured me that palms and passion coexist.

She whispered, "Jim, I have learned so much during this struggle. I have learned what it means to be scared, to fear something bigger than myself. But I have also learned the value of true friends and good doctors and honest prayers." (Did you hear it? Palms and passion.)

"I have learned," she continued, "that I am not immune from the worst that life has to offer. But I know that I can face it with a unique Christian joy." (Did you hear it? Palms and passion.)

This is a day—a holy day—that teaches us we cannot simply compartmentalize our lives. Instead, we have to live our lives courageously, during the best of times and the worst of times, even when it all seems to happen at the same time. The only way to make sense of our lives is to live them in the presence of and under the guidance of and within the care of Jesus Christ, who knows how it feels to experience palms and passion...together.

THE TRUTH IS SENSATIONAL ENOUGH

EASTER SUNDAY
MARK 16:9–20

It's called the longer ending of Mark. The oldest manuscripts of Mark's gospel stop at verse 8. Admittedly, it's a bit plain, even dark. The last word of the oldest ending is "fear."

For the first few years and decades after the death and resurrection of Jesus, these short, plain, dark verses seemed to be adequate. But as other gospels began to emerge—with all their detail, drama, and retrospective glory—Mark needed something. So someone (inspired by God, I'm sure) added verses 9–20—the longer ending of Mark. In this longer ending, Mary Magdalene testifies, Jesus makes appearances, and the disciples are instructed to prove their faith by handling snakes, speaking in tongues, exorcising demons, and drinking poison. For those who needed a more exciting, more sensational ending, that ought to do it.

I'm not sure who was being interviewed on National Public Radio, but his question concerning the media's role and influence in our culture caught my attention. Rhetorically probing his chosen profession, he asked, "Why do we attempt to sensationalize every story when the truth is sensational enough?"

I thought to myself, "That would be a good question for the church to ask. Every event, every service, every year does not have to be more and more sensational!"

We held our annual Children's Easter egg hunt yesterday. There was a huge crowd as usual, and probably no larger than usual. Several people commented, however, that this event just keeps getting bigger and bigger every year.

No, it doesn't, I silently—very silently—thought to myself. We have this need, however, to believe that it gets bigger and bigger. In fact, as our children were searching for the coveted "golden egg" (a spray-painted plastic egg crammed full of even more decadent candy delights than a pink or blue or green plastic egg—how's that for sensational?), one of our adults playfully commented, "Next year we'll have to hide a platinum egg!"

We feel this need to get bigger and bigger and better and better and more and more sensational. I'm not immune.

Our church is blessed to have a host of ordained persons as part of the congregation. With a religious university, a religious publisher, and a religious convention office within the city, we have our fair share of ordained parishioners. I have found them to be true friends, confidants, and able sounding boards for the content of my thoughts, prayers, and sermons. They have pushed me to be a better minister. And yet, they have always welcomed me as their minister. Fellow pastors have observed that they would feel intimidated preaching before such a crowd. It doesn't bother me...usually. Again, I'm not immune.

I picked up today's order of service and saw that one of our ordained members would be offering the morning invocation. I commented to my secretary, "Looks like I will have to rewrite my sermon."

"Why?" she asked.

"Because Scott prays better than I preach," I sarcastically responded.

I'm not immune. If Scott is praying, then the sermon has to be a little more sensational.

How did the National Public Radio guest ask it? Why do we attempt to sensationalize every story when the truth is sensational enough?

It's a question the church needs to ask. We harbor this incessant need to "one up" ourselves every year. Lent, Palm Sunday, Easter, Advent, and Christmas. They have to be a little better than last year. They have to be a little more sensational or people might not come…people might not believe.

A friend of mine served on the staff of a large church in the North Atlanta area several years ago. Their church produced a live Passion Play each Easter season. It had started simply enough—children in bathrobes with Nike sandals. But each year, it became increasingly elaborate. The bathrobes were set aside for tailored costumes. Children were eventually replaced with trainable adults. Live animals eventually joined the cast. And then came the forklift…

They had been crucifying Jesus for years. But they had never concocted a method for resurrecting each season's Savior…until the forklift. Hidden behind a papier-mâché tomb, with smoke machines churning smoke, the massive machine lifted Jesus to a victorious height of 12 feet above the tomb. As the choir sang their rousing finale at full throttle, Jesus discreetly disappeared (was driven away) into the darkness.

You know me. I had to ask my friend, "How do you discreetly 'crank' a forklift in the middle of a play?"

"Oh, we worked that out," he responded. "An offstage narrator says, 'and then there was a great earthquake.' The forklift is cranked and Jesus is lifted from the tomb."

"You're kidding."

"Well, it sort of sounds like an earthquake," he sheepishly responded.

I'm sure they will do it a little better next year—a little more sensational. How did the NPR guest say it? Why do we attempt to sensationalize every story when the truth is sensational enough?

I'm glad we gather every Easter morning in the quiet of this sanctuary. We don't handle snakes or drink poison or exorcise demons. We sing familiar hymns and tell an old familiar story. It's a simple story that assures us of peace amid chaos, life amid death, and hope amid darkness. There's no need to sensationalize it because the truth is sensational enough.

MISCELLANEOUS LITURGICAL DAYS

A God Begrudged

Pentecost Sunday
Matthew 20:1–16

I don't like this parable. I have grown up in a world that takes seriously issues of seniority and tenure and justice and fairness. While these ideals are not always achieved, they are at least valued in my world. This parable does not set well with me. It goes counter to what I think and believe. My guess is that, deep down, you don't like it either. You probably just wouldn't say it.

Dan Miles would say it. Dan Miles. God rest his soul. I loved him and the old coot actually loved me—a rare sentiment between him and preachers. Dan died during my tenure as pastor of the First Baptist Church in Baxley, Georgia. I preached his funeral. I never read this parable and not think of Dan.

One summer Sunday morning, I read this parable as part of our worship and then referenced it within the body of my sermon. Dan shook my hand and shook his head after the sermon. "Jesus was just wrong!" he firmly asserted.

You have to understand: Dan had his own view of justice. Stories of Dan's unique view of life were rampant in the apocryphal lore of Baxley. Were they true? Who knew? We told them over and over again, just the same. My favorite involved a car accident. Dan allegedly backed out of his driveway and onto Main Street. An approaching car, with no time to stop, hit Dan. The police were summoned and, after arriving and assessing, filed a report listing Dan as the party at fault. Dan decided to contest the ticket in court, or as he liked to put it, to fight the charges. Dan's defense? "I've been backing out of the driveway the same time of day for years. She should have known I was coming out!"

Dan shook my hand and shook his head that morning and determinedly said, "Jesus was just wrong!" I'm not going to say that Jesus was wrong. But I'm going to say, again, that this parable makes me a little uncomfortable. If I had been in the vineyard all day and someone else had only been there one hour, and at the end of the day we got the same pay, I'd be thinking, *Where was his lazy self all day long while we were working?*

Pope John Paul II had a wonderful spirit and a wonderful wit. In an interview, he was once asked, "Exactly how many people work at the Vatican?" He quickly responded, "About half of them."

This parable forces me to struggle with how I feel about certain people. I have a problem with people who will not work or do not work. I resent people who slip in on the end of a job or slip in on the end of a project and get the same glory and the same credit and the same reward as those who have struggled from the beginning.

I used to hate going to youth camp. Our church's summer youth camp was held at Siloam Springs, Arkansas. The setting was beautiful. The teachers were a delight. It was the evening worship I couldn't stand. Each evening, a young person was chosen to share a testimony during the worship service. Without fail, the camp directors always chose someone who was just saved the night before or who had just became a Christian a week or two earlier. Inevitably, they had always smoked things or drank things or done things that I had purposefully, faithfully avoided all my life. They had loved Jesus for a few hours or maybe loved him for a few days. I had loved Jesus for as long as I could remember. Somehow, growing up in church wasn't quite as exciting as throwing up after parties. So they always got to share their testimonies. I just sat there in the congregation while they spoke. We all got a day's wage.

We mentally and figuratively deal with this injustice by construing heavenly reward systems in our minds. We imagine a final judgment where crowns and their inset stars reflect the strength of our character and the cumulative (as well as comparative) worth of our good behavior. Those testimonial selectees have received their reward on earth. Wait till they see my crown! It's our attempt to make life fair, to make faith fair, perhaps to make this parable fair. As long as my final reward is better than theirs, well, you get the picture.

Of course, deep in our hearts we know better, don't we? That last-minute, repentant thief on the cross is going to be living in the same paradise you and I will call home. He might even be my roommate. It just doesn't seem fair. Why can't God build a little equity into the system? Which takes me to another level of discomfort.

This parable is not really about how we look at each other. Its meaning is slyly exposed in those final verses that are often overlooked. The parable itself is so difficult that it's hard to get past payday! When all the wages have been distributed, however, the landowner responds to the sense of injustice experienced by the tenured laborers. "Do you look at me with an evil eye?" he asks. "Do you begrudge me because I'm generous?"

This parable is not just addressing how I feel about other people. At a much deeper level, *this parable forces me to consider how I feel about God.* I'm serving a God who welcomes me to his vineyard with the promise, "I'm going to pay you what is right at the end of the day." And at the end of the day, he pays us all the same. No matter how hard I work. No matter how hard I try. No matter how my life compares to the best or the worst of the population. We get paid the same. I want to scream, "That's not fair!"

I'm not the first to question the fairness of God, so I don't feel too bad. The prophet Habakkuk observed the injustices of life. In his ancient city, the evil got wealthier and wealthier and the good folk got poorer and poorer. He cried out, "It's not fair!"

Ethan the Ezrahite, an obscure priest, cries out to God in Psalm 89, "You promised to protect us and love us and keep us for all generations. But now the heathen Babylonians have come and destroyed all that we had. It's not fair!"

A young couple sat in my office about twelve years ago. They wanted children. They had prayed for children. They tried to have children—all to no avail. They sat in my office and asked, "Why? We are good people. We have been good from our childhoods. We have tried to be faithful, responsible adults. We haven't sown wild oats. We've been in church all of our lives. We have worked hard to provide a good home for each other and our children. But there have been no children. God seems to be giving plenty of children to people who don't want them or don't care for them or even mistreat them. Jim, it's not fair!"

And then there is this parable. Those latecomers wasted the whole day—wasted their lives for all we know—but in the end, they got the same wage. We could belabor these injustices all day long, but at the end of the day, we'd all still get the same wage. So why don't we just wrap this up?

Here's my final word on the parable: God is rarely fair, but God's lack of fairness heavily leans toward grace. Grace, by definition, is not fair.

I like the way the old Sunday school teacher defined grace. "Grace is the break you get when you don't deserve it. And you'll never understand it and never appreciate it until you need it."

I'm not really comfortable with this parable. But when all is said and done, I know me, and I'm glad God is more gracious than fair. The real reward of our life is not what or how much we get from God, particularly as it is compared to other people. The greatest joy of life is simply being invited to live and work in the vineyard, to be in the presence of God.

It's like the little child who followed his mom around all day long. She would go to the kitchen and he would hop up in a chair beside her. She would go to the living room and he would find his way to the sofa. She would go to the bedroom and he plopped down beside her on the bed. Walking down their hallway, she almost tripped over him as he shadowed her to her next destination. "Is there something you need?" she asked. He looked up and said, "No, ma'am, I just wanted to be with you."

The greatest reward of this life it is not how much we get or what kind of reward we receive. It is simply being invited to be a part of vineyard—being in the presence of God. And I guess we should say the more the merrier, regardless of when or how they come.

I Confess: I'm Confused

Trinity Sunday
Romans 5:1–5

I have spent more than forty years in Sunday school, four years in a state university, three years in a Baptist seminary, three more years in a Presbyterian seminary, and have attended numerous conferences and continuing education events. I have read more books and have endured more lectures than one life span ought to allow...and I'm still confused.

The Trinity always does that to me. God the Father, God the Son, God the Holy Spirit...three in one...separate but the same...Jesus sitting at the right hand of his Father while the Spirit dwells in us—but they are all the same. Or how about *Jesus* praying to the *Father* just before he breathes the *Spirit* onto his disciples, and yet, they are all the same?

Today is Trinity Sunday. I confess: I'm still confused.

It was several weeks before Easter and a local radio station had advertised that the Easter bunny was going to be at the Sears Catalogue store. I had seen several rabbits in my lifetime—many in my own yard. But I had never seen the Easter bunny. My siblings and I were excited about the trip to Sears and the planned encounter. We hopped into my mom's '69 Buick and headed off to Sears.

When we walked in, there he was! You couldn't miss him. A big, white, furry creature seated in a whicker chair. If he had stood, he would have been more than six feet tall—seven feet tall if you counted the ears. He was nothing like the bunnies in our backyard. We were scared to approach him—and scared not too. He held in his hand the power to give or withhold a precious commodity—the Easter basket. So, timidly, we approached and we sat in his lap.

With a strangely familiar voice, he asked, "What do you want for Easter, little boy?"

I told him I wanted candy eggs, but not the white mushy kind. I wanted the malted chocolate eggs. I also wanted lots of jellybeans, but no licorice-flavored jellybeans. I also wanted a chocolate bunny, the solid kind, not the hollow kind. And I said it would be nice if a toy or two were in the basket as well—preferably plastic army men.

He laughed a very familiar laugh. He rubbed me atop my head. I walked away.

Romans 5:1 says we have been justified by faith. We are at peace with God the Father. That's good news. It's good news because this God that we call Father is larger than life. Go ahead, read your Bible from Genesis to Revelation. You will find that when God loves, God loves deeply. When God forgives, God forgives completely. And when God gets angry, you don't want to be anywhere around.

This magnificent God that we call Father is also a shepherd and a king and a warrior and a nursing mother. He is wind and fire, cloud and wisdom. This God that we call Father is bigger than life. We are scared to approach him and scared not too. He holds in his hand the power to give or withhold the most precious of commodities—life.

It was several weeks after Easter; it may have been Trinity Sunday morning, but I can't be sure. My dad was moving through the normal Sunday morning routine—ritually polishing his three sons' shoes. Having buffed a high shine on the three pair of elementary-school-sized loafers, he asked me to go get his shoes out of his closet. We rarely went into our parents' bedroom, and even rarer did we see the inside of their closet. I opened the door to what seemed a cavernous dark hole. On hands and knees, I crawled across steel-toed work boots and tennis shoes. Reaching the far right side of the closet, I laid my hands on dad's heavy black wingtips. And that's when I saw them dangling at the far end of the closet, white and furry. I confess: I was confused.

This mysterious basket-bearing being was a little more human than I originally thought. This newly revealed mixture of flesh and blood and fur sent my head spinning.

On the other hand, however, it all started to make sense. I always got the right candy in my basket even if no one else in the whole elementary school did. And every year I would receive a gift in my basket. Now it all made sense. As I sat in the bottom of that closet, wingtips in hand, I thought to myself, *I am one well-connected kid!*

Romans 5:1–2. We have peace with God the Father through Christ Jesus, through whom we have received access to the grace in which we stand. Our Lord Jesus Christ is the fleshy side of God. In the person of Jesus Christ, we saw God weeping at the tomb of Lazarus because he was sad. In the person of Jesus Christ, we saw God go to the mountains to rest because he was tired. In the person of Jesus Christ, we saw God bow in a garden and pray because he was in agony; He knew what it was like to hurt. Through Jesus Christ, God knows what we think and what we feel. That is why God is so incomparably capable of giving us what we need—because he knows. So today, I can sit on any pew in any church and think to myself, *Through Jesus Christ, I'm one well-connected kid.*

It was years later that I learned my dad was a seasonal employee at the Sears Catalogue store and one of the Easter bunny's helpers. Like most kids, I didn't fully understand my father. I do cherish, however, what he gave me. I cherish what he gave our little community—through his presence at the Sears store—during the holidays. The spirit that he brought to that little town by humbly putting on a shell with which he was not comfortable, well, I think you understand.

I will never forget standing in line to see the Easter bunny at the Sears store. Of course, I wasn't the only person in line. Yee Wing was in line; his dad owned a grocery store in town. Michael was in line; he was my across-the-street neighbor. John was in line; he was my across-the-tracks neighbor, but he was a good friend nonetheless. Tab was in line; his parents owned most of the buildings in our little town (at least that's what the Easter bunny said). Debbie was in line; I don't think her parents owned anything. We were all standing in together, talking and playing and dreaming. Our parents were standing beside us. They were huddled and conversing at one of the few places that ever brought them together—the Easter bunny line. For one moment in time, we all shared the same excitement and the same hope and the same joy and the same expectation. My dad had brought that spirit to our little community.

Romans 5:5. God's love has been poured into our hearts through the Holy Spirit that has been given to us. Last week was Pentecost. We celebrated the power of the Holy Spirit to make us witnesses in the world. But today's text is not concerned with the Spirit's power in the world. In today's text, we learn that one of the roles of the Holy Spirit is to connect us, to bind us together within the church. It is this unifying love that allows us to be credible and powerful witnesses in the world.

The annual family picnic was going well until someone looked around and realized that little three-year-old Suzie was missing. Family and in-laws and invited guests were quick to begin their search. The gathered mass split into small search parties and casually looked for her around the farm, in the house, and in the adjacent fields. When thirty minutes had passed, and then an hour, and then two hours, the casual search turned into panic.

The sheriff's department was called. The cars of neighbors and friends began wheeling down the dirt road toward the farm. Everyone started calling each other and word got around. Before too many more minutes had passed, it seemed the whole community had arrived at the farmhouse. The local firemen were there. The bank president was there. Lawyers, lumberjacks, factory workers—even the town drunk was there. People of every color and every creed had converged on this one farm—scattering through the fields—to look for little Suzie.

After another unsuccessful hour of searching, one participant suggested that everyone hold hands. The volunteers would make one long line across the yard and move out into the fields. The randomness of their early search had no doubt left some small plot of ground untouched. By holding hands and walking together, no area would be overlooked.

It did not take long for them to come upon her lifeless little body. She had been bitten by a snake hours before. If she had been found a little earlier, maybe she could have lived. Her dad sat on the cool wet grass and rocked her little limp body. The only thing he said, over and over again, was, "I wish we had held hands sooner."

We have allowed too much to divide us in this world. There has been too much exclusion in the life of the church, too much exclusion in the life of denominations, too much "us/them" language in our own congregation. While there are a lot of things that confuse me about the Trinity, there is one thing of which I am absolutely certain—God the Father (who loves us) and Christ the Son (who saves us) and the Holy Spirit (who fills us) all want us to hold hands, to come together despite our differences, and rescue the lost children of this world. They want us to be one even as they are one. That part of the Trinity isn't confusing at all.

I Confess: I'm Still Learning

Transfiguration Sunday
2 Kings 2:1–14

Don Parker knew I was terrible with directions. He knew I had a short attention span, and he knew that the train of thought traveling on my one-track mind was easily derailed. All it took was one question, one comment, one conversation. So as we made our way down the escalator into the MARTA station, he kept asking me questions and engaging me in what seemed like a minutia of conversation, until we walked across the platform where the train would arrive. He kept on talking and kept on questioning until finally the train pulled up. The doors opened and the passengers got off. I stepped into the train, grabbed a handrail, and turned around just as the doors closed. Don stood outside smiling and waving as the train took me away. I rode one station down, got off, got on the train coming the other way, and rode back to where I started. Don was still standing there waving and laughing. As I got off he said, "You know, you really need to pay attention to where you are going—that was the wrong train." He had done it on purpose.

Dr. Don Parker was my mentor. I was fresh out of seminary, he was the senior pastor at First Baptist Church in Marietta, and he was a very competent, very compassionate man—except in MARTA stations. I often plopped down in his office and wore out my welcome by hounding him with questions about ministry, preaching, administration, and funerals. Knowing my schedule today, I'm not sure how he ever found time for me, but he did. During our years together in Marietta, he taught me about two extremes of ministry. I have since discovered they are the two extremes of life and faith as well.

On the one extreme, there are those things that are manageable. These are the routine, predictable parts of life that we all deal with day in and day out. *On the other end of the spectrum lies the extreme called the mysterious.* These are the wilderness moments that are often painful, never controlled, and sometimes insightful.

Elisha loved his mentor Elijah about the same way I loved Don Parker. Read 2 Kings 2. Throughout the chapter, I believe Elijah was trying to teach Elisha about these same two extremes. Elisha, a young prophet who was learning from Elijah, learned that there is a part of life that is manageable. In 2 Kings 2:1–7, Elisha is traveling with his teacher, Elijah. They go first to Gilgal and then to Bethel and then to Jericho and then to the Jordan. Each step along the way, they encounter companies or schools of prophets who come out to meet Elijah. Elijah is obviously their teacher. This is a route and routine that Elijah had followed for most of his life. In fact, a quick reading of 1 Kings will highlight the fact that Elijah traveled the circuit to Gilgal and Bethel and Jericho and the Jordan over and over again. It was a part of the routine of his life as he managed these schools of prophets. In today's text, Elijah is taking his farewell tour. It's his last visit in all of these places, and he discourages Elisha from tagging along. He tells Elisha, "There is no reason for you to come today—you stay here." Why didn't Elijah want Elisha to come? Who knows? Maybe he figured that Elisha had already been there before and had already learned all the lessons one can learn from going to Gilgal, Bethel, Jericho, and the Jordan. I'm convinced that Elisha wasn't through learning. In fact, if there was anything else to learn, it was that even the manageable routines of life are ordained and blessed by God.

Don Parker was a good mentor, particularly in what we might call the manageable moments—the predictable routines of life. When I had been the associate pastor and youth minister at First Baptist

Marietta for about a month, I was sitting in my office waiting on the big assignment. I thought that certainly at some point Don was going to call me and say, "I need you to do a Sunday morning stewardship sermon." Or maybe even, "You better start preparing now because Christmas is in six months and we want you to do the big Christmas sermon."

The buzzer finally rang on my phone and I picked it up. Don called me to his office and I ran over to get the big assignment. I sat down and he said, "I thought of something I need you to do."

I thought, *Here it comes.*

He said, "I want you create a schematic of the Sunday school classes in all three of our buildings. Be sure to list all the teachers' names that go with every room."

He must have seen the look on my face that said, "I went to seminary for three years to do that?"

Because he continued, "Jim, if you do this, you will not only acquaint yourself with every class in the three buildings of this complex, but you will also know every teacher. Then, when guests walk into our facility, you will know exactly where to send them. I want you to do this for me and for you."

My facial expression didn't change much, and that is when he said, "Jim, good administration allows for good ministry."

I did a lot of administration during those four years. I never got to preach a Christmas sermon—that was always Don's. But during our four years together, he mentored the manageable. He was the master of manageable moments.

Elisha and I have both learned that there is a part of life and a part of ministry that is manageable. These seemingly mundane moments and tasks are holy in and of themselves. We have also had to learn that there is a part of life that is mysterious. Elijah's routine management tour ends in verse 7 when Elijah and Elisha and some prophets come to the Jordan River. If you were listening closely to the story, you know that nothing that happens after verse 8 is routine at all. Elijah walks to the edge of the Jordan River, touches it with his mantle, and the waters part. Yes, Moses had done this before and Joshua had done this before, but it was still far from routine. Once they walk into the wilderness on the other side of the Jordan River, they encounter a whirlwind and chariots and horses and fire. That is not routine to say the least. That is the part of life that is mysterious. Elijah took Elisha across the Jordan River into the wilderness. It's the place where prophets confront the mysterious part of life—the part that cannot be managed.

Dr. Parker took me across the Jordan River into several wildernesses. He moved me into some moments for which seminary doesn't prepare you. He took me to some people and to some places that could not be predicted or managed.

A lady came in off the street one day in Marietta and made her way to Don's office. She sat down and claimed to be demon possessed. He listened to her for a few moments, looked up, and finally said, "You know, we have a new young minister here at our church, and he specializes in demon possession." He walked her across to my office, and he led me across the Jordan River into the wilderness of caring for those who have a mental illness.

One day, as Dr. Parker and I were leaving the office together, we met a homeless man at the door. We were locking up and the gentleman asked us for five dollars. Showing off my administrative savvy that I had been learning at First Baptist in Marietta, I explained to him our procedures and assured him that he would get some food if he would come back during the appropriate hours. I told him that we never handed out cash. Looking at Dr. Parker for some nod of affirmation—an indication that I had gotten all of the verbiage right—I saw Dr. Parker reach into his pocket, pull out a five-dollar bill, and give it to the man. The man left. Of course, thinking that this was a learning experience, I responded, "You don't know what he is going to do with that money. He could go and buy liquor for all you know." Dr. Parker responded, "What he does with the money is between him and God. Whether or not we give it is between us and God." He crossed the Jordan with me and walked me into that wilderness of learning how to care for the poor.

Late one afternoon, Don and I sat in the den of a dear lady of our church while her husband's lifeless body was still in the bedroom just down the hall. These weren't just parishioners, but good friends of Dr. Parker's. I think it was the first time that I had ever seen Don cry. We left the house after scripture reading and prayer, and we got into his Chevy Celebrity. He just stared at the steering wheel. After what seemed like an eternity, he said, "Sometimes ministry hurts." He walked me across the Jordan River into a wilderness of pain.

Some of his lessons were hard. Some of them may be even cruel. But, because of his lessons, I am much more comfortable and much more compassionate about the mysteries of life.

We all have people in our lives who are larger than life. Elisha had Elijah, I had Don, you had your teachers and your professors and your parents and drill sergeants and officers and coaches. These are the people who teach us about life and faith. They teach us that both the manageable and the mysterious are holy. Once they have handed us their mantles, it's time for us to go and be responsible for teaching others the same thing. But I confess: I'm still learning.

HOW WILL WE BE REMEMBERED?

Stewardship Sunday
Mark 14:1–11

"Do you know this place?" asked the ghost.

"Know it?" Scrooge joyfully exclaimed. "I apprenticed here! And look! There's old Fezziwig. He had the power to render us happy or unhappy—make our life a pleasure or a toil. He was always so generous to us!"

"He spent only a few pounds of your mortal money," said the ghost.

"Yes, but I remember the joy that he brought to all of us," said Scrooge.

It's called hyperbole—to exaggerate an idea in order to make a point. It's the practice of pushing a caricature as far as you can in order to teach a lesson. Dickens uses this literary technique well in his celebrated holiday classic, *A Christmas Carol*. The generosity of Fezziwig, who would open and empty his coffers at Christmastime in order to bring happiness to family and friend, is juxtaposed with the penny-pinching, miserly Scrooge who brings happiness to no one—not even himself.

Allow me to use a little hyperbole today. Allow me to exaggerate just a little bit, in the sermon, in order to make a point. After all, that's what preachers usually do without permission, right?

Mark 14 leaves itself wide open to this hyperbolic approach to interpretation. In this biblical chapter, we are presented with two different ways of giving—as different as Scrooge and Fezziwig in the

Dickens text. These two methods of giving might easily be labeled stewardship and generosity.

Let's begin by discussing stewardship. This is where most of us began our giving journey. For years, preachers have stood before us in the autumn months of the year and encouraged us to participate in stewardship campaigns. They told us that everything belongs to God. Everything we possess belongs to God. Everything we have ever had or will have belongs to God. We are just stewards of God's stuff. We are managers of God's assets, and we'd better manage it wisely. Of course, part of managing it wisely is our ability to relinquish sizable quantities of it to the church.

The whole idea of stewardship sets pretty well with us. It seems biblical, after all. There are two or three parables that introduce us to the idea and image of being stewards of God's talents or stewards of God's kingdom. Not only does it seem biblical enough, but it also fits nicely into our American economic culture. We prize the role of the manager—someone who can efficiently care for someone else's business—a good steward.

By the way, that is an important concept to understand when embracing the idea of stewardship—taking *care* of someone else's stuff. Don't move on too quickly. The good steward, the good manager, takes *care* of the owner's stuff. Great *care* must be taken with another person's properties. We have to be *careful* when handling the assets of another. "Careful" becomes a definitive character trait in the life of the good steward.

I have several friends who own trucks, and I refuse to borrow them. All of my friends have offered—time after time—the use of these vehicles. I always refuse. I choose instead just to throw the fertilizer bags, topsoil bags, and landscaping stone into the trunk of my little car.

They will often insistently argue with me, saying, "Don't haul that stuff in your car! Borrow my truck. Go ahead; it's just a truck. It doesn't matter if it gets dirty or gets a few scratches on it. It was meant to haul stuff. It's just a truck!" At least that's what they say.

I was standing in the front yard of one of our parishioners a few years ago. He was leaning against his truck, affectionately rubbing the driver's side wheel well, and he said, "There are two things in this world I love—my wife and my truck. You can borrow my wife if you want to." He laughed and then said, "I'm just kidding. You can borrow my truck anytime you want to."

I don't think so.

You know what it's like to drive someone else's car. We nervously, carefully make sure we return it in the condition we received it—if not better. We fill the tank, wash it, vacuum it, watch the miles, and avoid parking or driving anywhere that bumps and dents and nicks and scratches might be incurred. It's someone else's stuff and you know you have to give it back to them in good condition.

That's an interesting phrase, isn't it? "*Give* it back to them." Give? We're not giving anything. We're simply returning something that doesn't belong to us. We can't give it if it isn't ours. Therein lies the problem with the concept of stewardship. Stewards do not give. Stewards have nothing to give. The best a steward can do is to care for and return what belongs to someone else. If we are simply stewards, then whether we are returning a truck or returning a tithe, we are doing it because we have to, ought to, are required to, are obligated to. That's what stewards do. Stewardship is not about giving. Stewardship is about managing what is not yours.

While Jesus was in Bethany at the home of Simon the leper, a woman came with an alabaster jar of costly ointment. She broke the jar and lovingly poured the fragrant contents over Jesus' head. The disciples—all good stewards—complained about the waste. There were other ways this resource could have been used. Breaking, spilling, wasting—that's no way to handle someone else's stuff. And after all, everything we own belongs to God. She was scolded for her poor stewardship.

On the one hand there is stewardship, and on the other hand there is generosity. Irrational, careless generosity. The disciples scolded this woman because of her irrational, careless generosity. They preferred that she carefully, and without waste, fulfill her managerial obligation to sell the valuable resource, assign the profits to the appropriate line item, and funnel it to the poor. That would be good stewardship.

Jesus, however, hushed them. Why? Because she had brought the most valuable item she owned and carelessly, irrationally, given it to her Lord. Not because she had to or was obligated to or was required to, but because it was hers to give...and she wanted to.

I am about to set you free. Are you ready? I am truly going to set you free. I know this is a dangerous thing, but I'm going to do it anyway. I'm going to tell you something that no other pastor has probably ever told you. Are you ready? Here goes. All of your stuff is your stuff. It's yours. It belongs to you. You can do whatever you want to with it. It doesn't belong to God. You don't owe God anything.

(Go ahead. Take a breath. I'll wait.)

I challenge you to read your Bible and read it carefully. God has given us an abundance of gifts. The Bible teaches us that life is a gift. Eternal life is a gift. All of the blessings of life are gifts from God. Now, if there are strings attached, then they aren't truly gifts. But there are no strings. It's your stuff. You can do with it whatever you choose. It's your house. It's your car. It's your family. It's your money. It's all yours. I know that last year, during our annual stewardship sermon, I told you it was God's stuff. I was wrong. It's all yours.

You're still not breathing, are you? Let me put your mind at ease. For every biblical verse you can show me that says we are stewards, I can show you twenty that say you are God's child, an heir with Christ, and a recipient of the free gifts of God. It all belongs to you. You are truly free to do with it whatever you wish.

It is only in the context of this reality that we can become givers. Do you understand what I am saying? Now we are free to *give*, not just *return* something that does not belong to us. You can stop being careful. You can stop being so rational about every penny. You can break it and you can pour it out. It is your gift to give.

Now we preachers, at the end of every sermon, like to drive our point home. We often do this with the use of a profound quote or story or poem—typically penned by someone more powerful or credible than ourselves. I personally like to end with the words of Billy Graham or Mother Teresa or C. S. Lewis or St. Francis—someone who has carried the weight of Christendom on their shoulders for a respectable amount of time.

Today, however, I'm pulling out the authoritative verbiage of Sam Kent. You all know Sam. He rambunctiously resides in the children's department of our church. This past Wednesday evening, he represented his preadolescent peers and shared a "stewardship testimony" during prayer meeting. His words took us away from the idea of stewardship, however, and ushered us toward the concept of generosity. If you missed it, allow me to share his story.

"My job is taking the neighbor's trash to the street every week," Sam said. "That's how I get my money. Then I give a tenth of my money to God. The rest of it I like to spend on video games and other stuff."

We all chuckled. He continued.

"Now I know what you're thinking. You're thinking I give that tenth to God because my mom tells me to. That's not true. I do it because I want to."

Did you hear what Sam said? He may be the most credible theologian in the church—*my* money, a tenth of *my* money, because I *want* to. There are a lot of good people who are good managers, but Sam is going to be remembered as a good and generous giver. There are a lot of people who are good managers. But Fezziwig was remembered as a good and generous giver. There are a lot of disciples who are good managers. But the woman at Bethany—of whom Jesus said, "For as long as the gospel is proclaimed in this world she will be remembered..."—will be remembered as a good and generous giver. What cheers God's heart the most is not when we give because we ought to or have to or need to or should. But when we give what is ours because we *want* to. And that's the difference between stewardship and generosity.

TELL US, JOHNNY GILBERT

All Saints' Day, November 1, 1998
Deuteronomy 34:1–12

You may not know Johnny Gilbert. You are probably familiar, however, with names like Bob Eubanks, Monty Hall, Wink Martindale, and Alex Trebek. All these people are beloved game-show hosts. But who is Johnny Gilbert? Allow me to refresh your memory with the turn of one phrase: "Tell us, Johnny Gilbert, what consolation prizes our runner-up contestant will take home today." That directive prompted a voice whose face we never see to reward contestants with coveted items like a year's supply of Rice-A-Roni (the San Francisco treat), an assortment of Maybelline products, and/or a freezer full of Freeze Pops. Everyone else had won refrigerators, living room furniture, and maybe even a car. But those poor runner-up contestants—who missed the bonus question—were sent home with Rice-A-Roni, cosmetics, and freeze pops.

That has to be one of the most disappointing moments in a person's life. To travel all the way to California, be selected for a game show, miss the bonus question, and then hear those ominous words, "Tell us, Johnny Gilbert...."

I wonder if Moses felt that way. Deuteronomy 34, in my opinion, is one of the most unfair texts in all of scripture. Moses had been obedient to God. At God's command, he went back to Egypt, called down plagues upon the Egyptians, led the Israelites out of Egypt, spent forty years wandering through a wilderness with the complaining congregation, and then he made one mistake.

In Numbers 20, the Israelites are thirsty. You remember the story. God instructs Moses to call forth water from the rock in the name of the Lord. But when Moses stands before the rock, he strikes the rock and calls for water in his own name. God's response? Moses is not allowed to enter the Promised Land. Moses made the long trip through the wilderness, got every other answer right, made one mistake, and, tell us Johnny Gilbert, what consolation prizes will Moses take home today? Deuteronomy 34, at face value, is one of the most unfair Scriptures in all of biblical literature. Often, however, there is more to scripture than face value. Maybe we need to look more closely at Moses' consolation prizes.

Moses never lost his health. Moses was 120 years old when he died. His sight was unimpaired and his vigor was unabated. I've heard people say on more than one occasion that if you have your health, you have everything. There are few things we dread more than the inevitable decline of health and mobility—losing the capacity to do and go and think on our own. But Moses' sight was unimpaired and his vigor unabated until the day he died.

It reminds me of a little seven-year-old boy who was celebrating his birthday. After the candles had been blown out, the traditional celebratory song sung, the cake eaten, and the presents opened, his mother asked him, "Well, how does it feel to be seven years old?"

Surrounded by presents, torn wrapping paper, cake crumbs, and friends, he responded, "It's great; the older I get, the better life gets!"

That's seven years old. It's harder to carry that same health and enthusiasm and optimism with us into the later years of life. Unless, of course, you're like Moses. He was 120 years old and in excellent health. That's not a bad consolation prize.

Moses had also gained the love of the people. After the death of Moses, the Israelites wept for thirty days. In some cultures, families pay mourners to attend the funerals of their loved ones. It creates the perception that the deceased was well loved and missed. Moses needed no professional mourners. These appear to be genuine tears from people who genuinely loved Moses.

For two years, my wife and I lived in Tatum Springs, Kentucky—population maybe 300. I had the privilege of serving as pastor of Mt. Olivet Baptist Church. We rarely had more than forty people in Sunday school and worship. We only celebrated one baptism during my tenure there. At times I felt my influence and purpose were minimal at best.

As those two years came to an end, I graduated from seminary and was called to another church. I drove to Marshall Shoemaker's home—our deacon chair—to share the news with him. Sitting in his living room, I told him another church had called me and in a month we would be moving. I apologetically reminisced about my time there. I stated some regret at the lack of any numeric growth. I wondered aloud if a more experienced, wiser minister might have brought maturity to the crises I had been forced to address. But before I could forge too far down that road, Marshall interrupted me and said, "Jim, we love you. You are the first pastor to actually live in the parsonage in over a decade. You came and lived among us. Every week, you prepared sermons and preached them as if there were two thousand in the congregation. You need to understand that we love you. It will hurt to see you leave, but we're proud you are moving on."

It is no small thing to be loved by people. I would imagine, in Moses' case, that was quite a consolation prize.

Moses was also able to mentor another in ministry. Our text says that Joshua, the son of Nun, was full of the spirit of wisdom because Moses had laid his hands on him. The Israelites obeyed Joshua just as they had obeyed Moses.

If you keep up with such things, we are in the middle of Georgia's deer season. Two years ago, I stealthily crept into the middle of a dark morning forest, climbed a deer stand, and waited for a treasured trophy to walk by. For the animal rights activists among us, as well as others who are disturbed by the sport of hunting, don't worry: the deer were in no danger. Yes, I had a gun and a scope and some camo and a deer stand and some bullets, but I assure you, the deer were in no danger. (I was once told I would see more deer if I stopped carrying crackers, a book, and a radio with me. I can't help it. I get bored easily.)

I sat in my tree stand waiting for almost an hour. The sun finally rose and I could clearly see the fields that surrounded this little stretch of wood. I could tell this was the morning. I was going to see a deer. That's when I saw it. Out of the corner of my left eye, I saw something move along the edge of a neighboring field. Leaning forward and squinting a bit, I could tell the moving object was not a deer. It was a young man. Maybe a fellow hunter, I thought.

I watched him lay a black case on the ground, and then he pulled not a gun but a trumpet out of the case. For the next hour, he broke into every football fight song one could imagine!

The next morning at church, I stopped our local band director in the hallway. I vehemently complained to him that I had spent weeks getting this spot ready for deer hunting. I had scouted for deer signs, picked the perfect tree, built the deer stand, and dreamed of this day. But when my big moment finally came, one of his students stepped out into the field and blared a bunch of noisy notes.

The band director looked at me with an insane look of excitement on his face. "Really?" he asked.

"Yes," I said, "It was terrible!"

"No," he responded, "this is great! He was really practicing his trumpet?"

The young boy had told the director that his parents were tired of him practicing in the house. It was far too loud. The director encouraged him to get up early on Saturday mornings and walk to the farthest end of their farm and play as loud as his heart desired.

"He actually took my advice," the director mused with great satisfaction. "It's good to know my leadership is finally paying off. By the way, what did you do when he started playing?"

"I opened a pack of crackers, pulled out my book, and listened for a while."

The band director was excited that something had finally taken root in that young man's life; he was practicing. It's no small consolation prize to pass on your values to those who come after you.

I'm often asked to identify the most satisfying part of my work as a minister. I usually respond with a listing of names: Don, Kevin, Joe, Kim, Mark, Jessica, and several others. They are all people whom I have had the privilege to watch enter the ministry. We've talked and prayed and worked together. I've listened to them and I think they've listened to me. It brings a lot of joy to my life to see them mature and succeed in ministry. It is no small consolation prize to pass your passion on to someone else.

Johnny Gilbert, Moses doesn't get the Promised Land, but what consolation prizes do you have for him? He gets his health. He gets the love of the people. He gets to mentor others in ministry. That is not a bad list. I must admit, however, that it still doesn't seem fair. All that work, all that obedience, all that time in the wilderness, but no Promised Land. Of course, there is one other consolation prize.

It was in the wilderness that Moses established his relationship with God. In the wilderness, Moses spoke with God *panim el panim*—face to face—as a man speaks with his friend. It was in the wilderness that Moses enjoyed the close presence of God. It was in the wilderness that Moses learned God's name, learned of God's power, and learned God's ways. It was in the wilderness that Moses learned that it's more important to get close to God than it is to get things from God.

So my guess is that the children of Israel got the Promised Land, but they never enjoyed what Moses had. Once the children of Israel enter Canaan, we rarely hear of milk and honey. We often hear of Hittites and Amorites and Philistines and wars and rumors of wars.

Moses wouldn't have traded his years in the wilderness for one day, one decade, or even a lifetime in the Promised Land. It was in the wilderness that Moses came to know, really know, God. Perhaps that's where we come to know God as well.

I can hear Moses echoing the words of Maya Angelou as he walked into the valley of Moab: "I wouldn't take nothing for my journey now."[2] Knowing God is not a bad consolation prize.

---

[2] Maya Angelou, *Wouldn't Take Nothing for My Journey Now* (New York: Random House, 1993).

ONE IMPRESSIVE SOLDIER

Veterans Day
Luke 7:1–10

The children were probably impressed with the gleam from the blade of his sword. It was a metal that had been so finely ground that it could sever life or limb from a man with one simple swing of the arm. Children are often enamored and impressed and intrigued by weapons and swords and light sabers and guns and the things they play with in their imaginations.

His peers, who served with him and under him, were probably impressed with his battle-scarred breastplate. It was polished to a high shine, and yet it bore the marks and gashes and scars that showed where swords and spears had missed their fatal mark. The indentions on his breastplate were like purple hearts for a battle-wise Roman centurion. There is no doubt about it; the soldier in his uniform was an impressive sight.

It wasn't the uniform of this centurion, however, that Jesus found impressive. We already know that God doesn't tend to look at the appearance of a person. What they look like and what they wear is not what impresses God. God looks at a person's heart. That is what impresses God. When God looks at this centurion in Luke 7, through the eyes of Christ, he is impressed by the soldier's faith. In fact, after hearing the words of this centurion, Jesus turns to the crowd following him and says, "You know, in all of Israel I haven't found faith like this."

What was it that made this centurion's faith so impressive to Jesus?

His faith had made him kind. Did you hear how the text describes this centurion over against all the other centurions we read about in the New Testament? In verse 2, it says he has a slave that he highly values. That value didn't have anything to do with money. It was a slave he loved and cared for and honored and respected. In verse 5, the Jews who came to talk to Jesus say, "You do not understand. This centurion is worthy of your care because he loves our people." In a time when most soldiers were known as barbaric and cruel, here is one who unashamedly showed love and concern to the Jewish citizens. Jesus is impressed when faith makes one kind.

Read the Scriptures closely and you will find that, in the kingdom of God, love and kindness are often the measuring sticks of true faith. In fact, if a person is narrow and hateful and judgmental and self-righteous, they may have a severe case of bad religion, but not faith.

Henry James, the great novelist, reportedly said to his nephew as James was dying, "There are only three things that are important in this life. Number one is to be kind. Number two is to be kind. Number three is to be kind. That's what matters in the living of a life."

Jesus looked at this centurion and saw that his faith had made him kind. Jesus was impressed with that kind of faith. *Jesus also saw that his faith had made him generous.* Did you hear what the people say at the end of verse 5? "He not only loves us, but this is the man who built our synagogue for us. He is a gentile—he can't even enter the synagogue. He gained nothing from this deal for himself (except maybe the grief of his peers for having built the synagogue for those Jews down in Capernaum). But he built our synagogue for us. He is a generous man." All great people of faith are. Generosity is one of the natural expressions of true faith.

I was driving through Atlanta some time ago, listening to the radio, when I heard the announcer say, "We'll give $1,000 to our tenth caller." I didn't know the number and didn't have a phone with me, so I couldn't call. Many other people must have called, however, because after the song was over the announcer started answering the phone live on the air. To caller after caller he said, "I'm sorry, you are the eighth caller." Then, "I'm sorry, you are the ninth caller."

Finally, he answered the phone and said, "You are our tenth caller!" Of course the voice on the other end of the line screamed, "I can't believe it! I can't believe it! I can't believe it!"

After the announcer finally got the caller settled down, he inquired, "What are you going to do with the money?"

She immediately responded, "The first $100 I'm going to give to my church."

I didn't hear another word she said. It was just that fast. She didn't think about it. She didn't hesitate or take time to pray about it. She simply reacted and acted according to the nature of her faith. She was generous with the things she received.

Jesus looked at this centurion who had built the synagogue for the Jews and was impressed with the generosity his faith had produced. But I think the primary reason his faith was so impressive goes beyond kindness and generosity. After all, anyone can muster a little kindness and generosity. *The real reason his faith was so impressive was because it had produced a humble trust.* There was a humility and trust in his life that I think stirred Jesus. Here was a man who readily confessed, "I'm used to giving orders. I tell somebody to go and they go. I tell somebody to come and they come. I tell somebody to do this and they do it." This is a man who was used to sipping wine with dignitaries, a man used to wielding power in the Roman provinces. But how does he explain himself in verses 6 and 7? He says, "Jesus, the reason I sent my servants to you is because I am not even worthy for you to come under my roof. I sent servants to you because I'm not even worthy to come and stand before you. Jesus, I know that if you just say the word my slave will be healed. In my own power, Jesus, I'm powerless. I'm used to giving orders, but this is an order I can't give." That's a humble trust.

On June 1, 1676, the Swedish Navy learned a lesson in humility and power. They launched a naval ship called the Cronin. I think the translation of that name in English is the "crown." It took them seven years to build the ship. One hundred twenty-two cannons were housed on board weighing a total of approximately 240 tons. It was the most powerful ship in the fleet. The minute it hit water, however, it sank under the weight of its 240 tons of guns—humility and power.

I think I'm a fair father. I hope I'm an adequate preacher and pastor. I've tried to be a good husband and prepared teacher. But there is not a week that goes by when I don't have to pray, "O God, help me prepare. Help me prepare Sunday's sermon. Help me prepare this class lecture. Help me prepare my children for the chapters that are coming in their future. Dear God, help me." I know if I rely on my own skills and my own power, I will surely sink.

I look out at this congregation and assume you are all fine parents. Many of you are wonderful businessmen and women, competent electricians and educators, doctors, lawyers, and servants in this community. But I can tell you this—if all you've got are your own cannons and you do not humbly, trustingly rely upon God in your life, you will surely sink. Jesus looked at this centurion, heard his words, and knew there was a humble trust in his life.

Margaret was going to undergo a medical procedure early one Friday morning. I rose before the crack of dawn, showered, got dressed, and drove to the hospital to be with her. When I got there, it was still dark. I entered her room and sat in the vinyl-covered chair beside her bed. She was asleep. After a few moments, she opened her eyes, looked over at me, wiped the sleep away, and said, "Jim, what are you doing here so early in the morning?"

I smiled and responded, "Well, I didn't want you to be alone when you went in for this procedure."

She smiled back at me and she said, "I wasn't alone." She had a humble trust in the power and presence of God in her life.

This is one impressive soldier in Luke 7. Not because of his bright battle-scarred armor. Not because of the gleaming sword that he carried at his side. Not even because of the power of his words. He is impressive because of his faith. A faith that made him kind. A faith that made him generous. A faith that made him trusting. And Jesus said, "You don't see faith like that very often."

EPILOGUE

The only thing that really matters in life is relationships; everything else is just stuff.

I spend my New Year's eves with the Swanson's, the Cassady's and the Morrow's. I have spent the last twenty plus Valentine Day's with a beautiful wife and three exquisite daughters. Easter lunch is shared with the Brown's, DuCharme's and Pierce's. On July 4, I step onto the streets of Atlanta with 54,999 other runners; we all know each other...in an ethereal kind of way. I've tricked and treated with the Glasgow's and the McCook's and the Souther's. Thanksgiving is reserved for the Fisher's—my in-laws. Christmas Eve finds me in a church filled with my faith family—too many friends to name.

We spend holidays and holy days with the people we love—friends and family. Because the only thing that really matters in life is relationships; the rest is just stuff.

Woven within the words of each of these sermons were the precious relationships of my life. I hope you've enjoyed meeting my family, friends, parishioners and, of course, my God. Each, in their own way, have pointed me...ushered me...pushed me...at times drug me...toward the truth. It's been a sensational journey thus far.

I've enjoyed sharing these holidays—and some of their inherent truths—with you. Thanks for welcoming me into the seasons of your life...